THE EGALITARIAN IDEAL AND THE AMERICAN HIGH SCHOOL

Research on Teaching Monograph Series

PUBLISHED

Student Characteristics and Teaching by
Jere E. Brophy and Carolyn M. Evertson

*The Invisible Culture: Communication in Classroom
and Community on the Warm Springs Indian Reservation*
by Susan Urmston Philips

*Pygmalion Grows Up: Studies in the Expectation
Communication Process* by Harris M. Cooper
and Thomas L. Good

Active Mathematics Teaching by
Thomas L. Good, Douglas Grouws, and Howard Ebmeier

Cooperative Learning by Robert Slavin

Class Size and Instruction by
Leonard S. Cahen, Nikola Filby,
Gail McCutcheon, and Diane W. Kyle

The Egalitarian Ideal and the American High School
by Philip A. Cusick

THE EGALITARIAN IDEAL AND THE AMERICAN HIGH SCHOOL

STUDIES OF THREE SCHOOLS

Philip A. Cusick

MICHIGAN STATE UNIVERSITY

Longman
New York & London

THE EGALITARIAN IDEAL AND THE AMERICAN HIGH SCHOOL
Studies of Three Schools

Longman Inc., 1560 Broadway, New York, N.Y. 10036
Associated companies, branches, and representatives
throughout the world.

LA
222
.C8
1983

Developmental Editor: Nicole Benevento
Editorial and Production Supervisor: Ferne Y. Kawahara
Manufacturing Supervisor: Marion Hess

Library of Congress Cataloging in Publication Data
Cusick, Philip A.
   The egalitarian ideal and the American High School
   Includes index.
   1. Education, Secondary—United States.
2. Educational equalization—United States.   3. Social values.
I. Title.
LA222.C8 1983   373.73   83-1159
ISBN 0-582-29015-5

Manufactured in the United States of America
Printing: 9 8 7 6 5 4 3 2 1   Year: 91 90 89 88 87 86 85 84 83

Contents

Preface   *vii*

1 Three Studies of Secondary Schools   **1**
   Introduction   1
   School Structure   4
   Methodology   6

2 Race, Discipline, and Attendance:
   The Basic Issues   **9**
   Introduction   9
   Biracialism in the Schools   13
   Discipline and Attendance   25
   Summary   41

3 The Curriculum, Part I   **43**
   Introduction   43
   The Curriculum of the Schools   44
   Teachers and Classes   48
   The Limits of Student Interest   68
   Summary   70

4 The Curriculum, Part II   **72**
   Introduction   72
   Creating Curriculum   73
   Teachers and Teachers   100
   Summary   103

5 Conclusion and Discussion   **104**
   Introduction   104
   Summary of the Argument: The Model   106
   Questions about the Model   113
   Implications of the Model   120

Appendix   Notes on Method   **131**
   Introduction   131
   Access to the Schools   135
   Some Particular Considerations   136

Index   *149*

Preface

Public schools are interesting because in them can be seen the dominant values of the society. The structure of the schools is not neutral but embodies just those values that it is designed to pass on. It reflects not only the values, but also the conflicts inherent in those values, conflicts between the new and the old, between the status quo and the need for change and between what people say they want and what they are willing to settle for. Just as the structure is tied to social values, so the behaviors undertaken by teachers, administrators, and students are connected through the structure to those same values and may also reflect the conflicts inherent in them.

This book is an account of some studies of three secondary schools. The subject of the studies is the behaviors of black and white students as they interact with each other, of teachers as they decide what to do in their classes and then carry out their decisions, of administrators as they go about their duties encountering the limits of their role. But the more important subject is the way those behaviors, the structure, and the social values that underlie the structure combine into a coherent and intelligible whole. The book is an attempt to consider these few secondary schools in all of their complexity.

The premise of the book is that the behaviors, structure, and social values combine into some coherent whole and the purpose of the book is to unravel the complexity of that whole. A secondary premise is that the complexity should be considered by those who wish to change the schools in ways that will lead to improved education for students. There is a problem with that secondary premise. Because the subject of the book is the complexity of the schools, it does not lend itself to the support of action suggestions or policy decisions of a type desired by many who are professionally concerned with schools. In fact, it tends to counter many of their suggestions by demonstrating that they may not take into account the full complexity of the situation.

It is all very well to advocate more rigorous standards, mandated literacy, increased graduation requirements, or harder-working teachers. But standards, graduation requirements, and the teachers' efforts are tied into the structure, which is tied back to the social values. These elements are not housed in vacuums nor reflective of simple individual idiosyncrasies. The common behaviors exhibited in the system are undertaken purposely or evolve in response to real constraints, constraints that affect the structure and hence the behaviors of the participants. It is a dilemma. To change and improve the schools, one needs a sufficient understanding of their complexity. But understanding their complexity may bind one into not knowing where to make the changes. However, that is a problem for the reader, not the writer.

My task is to use, describe, and explain the events I witnessed and account for them in terms of the structure and the values underlying that structure. If at times the explanation is complex, it is because the questions addressed are complex. Why are some (however few) teachers allowed to do nothing in their classes? Why must schools retain and continue to work with students who give repeated evidence that they are not interested in learning anything, let alone learning what the schools teach? How do teachers decide what to teach and why do they do such different things in their classes ?And why, no matter what a teacher does, is he or she allowed to justify it in terms of being "good for kids." Such questions are complex, but they lie at the heart of the school and the center of our educational processes, and for that reason they are worthy of our consideration.

There are a number of friends and colleagues who assisted with the research projects. Some helped with the initial proposals, some with the data collecting, and all to some degree assisted with the development and the writing. I would like to thank Robert Ames, Richard Ayling, Jere Brophy, Patrick Chianetta, Donald Crowder, Keith Goldhammer, Georganne Cusick, Janice Earle, Jack Francis, Barbara Gothard, Terry Havel, Anton Lingal, Judy Lanier, Barbara Markle, Donald McMillan, Donna Palmer, Ernest Russell, David Semrau, Lee Shulman, and Gary Sykes.

Philip A. Cusick

1

Three Studies of Secondary Schools

INTRODUCTION

The subject of this book is the structure of three public secondary schools; the thesis is that the keystone of that structure is their commitment to an American version of the egalitarian ideal, that is, to provide each student with an opportunity for social, political, and economic equality. The content of this book will be descriptions of classes, events, activities, and behaviors, supplemented by accounts of interviews with teachers, administrators, and students. From the descriptions and accounts will be developed an abstracted model of the structure common to those schools to explain my thesis that the key to that structure is the schools' commitment to that egalitarian ideal.

The three schools to be described all share the structure common to public secondary schools. They are founded on the same premises and share the same assumptions, staffing patterns, programmatic elements, operating procedures, and types of rules and regulations. They even evoke the same types of problems and the solutions to those problems are probably quite similar. Because of the similarity of these three to most secondary schools, that model may contribute to our understanding of secondary schools in general.

The studies took place in three high schools in the same large industrial metropolitan area. Each study was designed to answer some specific questions. The first was in a biracial, urban school of 1,900 students.[1] We undertook it to describe what black and white students do together and how what they do (or do not do) together affects other elements of the school. It was undertaken with Richard Ayling who, like me, had spent several years teaching in biracial urban schools and had also witnessed the tensions inherent in such places. At the time of the study, and for some years prior, these tensions increased considerably because of militancy on the part of blacks and resentment toward that militancy and toward forced integration on the part of whites. The reason behind that study was that while events outside the schools were pushing for or resisting desegregation, there was little general understanding of how black and white students accommodated (or, from our experience, failed to accommodate) one another on a daily basis within the schools. And there was even less understanding of how their interactions or the lack thereof affected other elements of the organization (e.g., teacher and administrative behavior, curriculum, activities, etc.). We selected a fairly large, biracial urban school, one that had a long history of bringing blacks and whites together, and pursued our questions through its classrooms and corridors for most of that year.

From that study we began to gain a better appreciation of the effects of biracialism and its potential for serious conflict. We understood what it did to the behavior of administrators and how and why they altered the administrative patterns of the school to accommodate it. We also understood what effects it had on the behavior of teachers, who were sometimes faced with sets of students nurturing an active dislike for one another, a dislike that could become inflamed into physical violence right in the classroom. The focus of attention in that study was on biracialism in an urban school. But we also understood that biracialism, as serious it was during that time of forced integration, was part of the larger problem of attendance and discipline. The school did not address the biracialism per se but treated it and its effects as part of the general problem of order, which is a major issue faced by all secondary schools. The focus of the study changed then from biracialism to the general problem of order in that urban secondary school.

The second study was undertaken in 1979 in two separate schools, also in the same metropolitan area.[2] One of these was a downtown school, population 2,400 students, with the same racial makeup as the school in which the earlier study took place. The other was a more suburban, all-white school located a few miles away, with 1,600 students, almost all of whom shared the same socioeconomic background as the students in the urban school. In that second study, the orienting questions centered around the development and implementation of the curriculum. Specifically, I wanted to know how teachers, singly or collectively, made decisions about what to do in their classrooms.

There are some particular events that made me curious about those processes. Since the late 1960s, there had been attempts by state departments of education and/or school boards and administrators to "rationalize" educational organizations with management techniques such as program evaluation review, management by objectives, planning programming budgeting systems, or accountability models of one sort or another.[3] All were designed to make schools conform to what were considered to be more intelligent management procedures. It certainly makes sense that if one is to more closely define the product (education), then one should have definite ways to manipulate the process (teaching). However, according to carefully conducted studies of some of these attempts, they succeeded in doing little other than increasing hostility between teachers and administrators. The administrators accused the teachers of insubordination or lack of sophistication, and the teachers accused the administrators of opportunism, ignorance, insensitivity, and highhandedness. As a result of the acrimony and general lack of success, many of these attempts were quietly (or not so quietly) dropped.

It was about that time and perhaps occasioned by the failure of many of those attempts that some adopted the idea that schools were really quite rational, but involved was a rationality of a different order.[4] Rather than thinking of them as management controlled, one had to think of them as loosely coupled organizations wherein events were purposely left unrelated to one another, supervision purposely left weak, and evaluation purposely left vague. To try to tighten and control those elements might raise questions about school processes, questions which are not only unanswerable but which, if asked, could diminish the high degree of public support and confidence that the schools currently enjoy. As this thesis, roughly stated, goes, the maintenance of public confidence and support is much more important than controlling internal processes, and the way that the schools are presently run is designed to optimize that essential public support. Furthermore, it is erroneous to think of schools as irrational just because they are less controlled internally than some would have them; rather, their organization is quite reasonable since it is designed to, and in fact does, accommodate political realities.

Given those two roughly conflicting ideas—first, that there is something anachronistic about the organization of schools because they continuously defy rational control, and second, that this defiance is functionally related to the maintenance of public confidence—I decided that specific descriptions of the processes that went on in secondary schools would be most useful. I reasoned that whatever rationality existed in those places could best be seen in the purposeful interactions of staff members as they went about their daily business, processing the affairs of the organization through their interactions.

As the study progressed, however, I found that the staff did not process the curriculum through their interactions. Rather each person was allowed, even encouraged, to develop his or her own content and approach to the subject matter, and was then allowed to deliver that curriculum to the students in ways that he or she deemed appropriate. More important to curriculum than collective agreement or mutual cooperation were the personal predilections of each individual teacher. What one decided to do or not to do in the classroom seemed to emanate not from consensually based, school-wide norms, but rather from how each individual, following his or her inclinations and predilections, decided to behave.

Therefore, just as the focus of the first study changed from biracialism to the more general area of attendance and discipline, this study changed from a focus on teacher networks to a study of the way individual teachers created their own professional lives. These four general themes (biracial-ism, attendance and discipline, creation of curriculum, and teacher lives) will serve as the vehicles through which a generalized model of the structure of these three secondary schools will be developed.

SCHOOL STRUCTURE

The premise of this book is that secondary schools have a structure and that any serious discussion of secondary education has to proceed from an understanding of that structure. The structure of an organization is an abstracted coherence that makes sense of the disparate elements. It is the set of events which turn upon themselves to complete and renew a set of activities. The structure is the realities of the place in terms of time, space, and resources and the set of values, behaviors, and understandings that the participants share about those realities. It serves as the base from which to judge certain activities and behaviors as worthwhile and to dismiss others as meaningless. The structure is what insiders have to accommodate to succeed, and what outsiders have to understand to appreciate the actions of insiders. It is the structure that confronts one when one enters an organization as either a staff member or a client. Regardless of his pre-dilections, ambitions, or talents, each person in an organization is faced with a set of constraints, and while each may make a different accom-modation, each has to accommodate and create his or her actions within those constraints.

The data comprising most of the book are taken from three separate schools, two of them urban and biracial, one all-white and suburban. While there are, of course, differences among the three, the thesis is all three share a similar structure and that general structure can be used to under-stand the behaviors and events that occur in those places. As the data are presented and the argument is pursued, the data from all three schools will be merged into an abstracted model of the general structure. An extension of the argument is that this abstracted structure is not limited to the three schools under discussion but may to a considerable degree be applied to most public secondary schools in America.

These three schools shared not only the same generalized task, they also shared with other secondary schools the same kinds of operating pro-cedures. They are publicly funded on a per pupil basis from local and state taxes. This makes them not only accountable to their paying public but also obligated to attract and retain all adolescents regardless of ability, ambition, or inclinations. That obligation results in a curriculum that is kept open, diverse, and fluid in order to continue to attract, retain, and interest all students. The definition of a high school education is therefore kept deliberately obscure and open to as many interpretations as there are combinations of courses. What is not obscure, however, is the heavy reli-ance on a bureaucratic organization with certified specialists, lines of authority, rules and regulations, and timed periods.

Underlying the three schools studied and all secondary schools is a firm belief that the acquisition of positive knowledge is or can be made interesting and appealing to everyone. By positive knowledge, I mean that which is generally accepted as having an empirical or traditional base, is socially useful, and lends itself to expression in verbalized and abstracted forms. It includes computer science, English literature, welding, and physical education. This is a very important assumption, because it justifies all the ways that the curriculum is diversified in order to appeal to students and in order to encourage each student to fulfill him- or herself.

Since schools are obligated to serve a large number of very diverse students in the same place, tremendous effort is needed to (1) insure attendance in school and (2) maintain order among this large and diverse population. The prevailing attitude among school administrators is that attendance is a more serious problem than are order and discipline. They feel that if they can attract the students into school and into class, then order will follow. Hence, in these and in all secondary schools, tremendous effort is directed toward reducing absenteeism, which in some urban schools can run as high as 30 percent on a given day, but in other schools may be as low as 3 or 4 percent. Low figures are maintained only by constant effort on the part of administrators. The impetus to retain students is strengthened by the funding processes and the belief about positive knowledge. If a student leaves, the school failed that student and the school loses funding. It is generally agreed upon by administrators and people who study schools that they are much more orderly than is commonly perceived. But it is also agreed upon that order and discipline are maintained at a very high cost, with the greatest part of the available administrative and supervisory help allocated to those areas.

There is an additional effect on administrators. Because of the school's publicness, administrators are obligated to spend a considerable amount of their time maintaining good relations with various segments of the community. While attendance and discipline may devour more time and energy in urban than in rural or suburban areas, maintaining good relations with the community is particularly time consuming in the latter, where the administrators spend a great amount of time assuring their wary communities that all is well with the schools.[5] This is not regarded as a "problem." Rather it is a fact of life when one is in charge of a publicly funded institution designed to serve the "needs" of all the citizens and open to influence by one or another of those citizens. But, just as attendance and discipline, it takes up a great amount of administrative and supervisory time. In fact, matters of attendance, discipline, and public relations take up the greatest part of the supervisory and administrative resources in public secondary schools.

In sum, while public secondary schools may be quite different from one another, some common elements are endemic to all, for example, large size, diversity, public and per pupil funding. From these come some additional elements, such as diversity, accountability, public influence, and a heavy commitment of resources to maintain good attendance, discipline, and public relations. The three schools I studied were separated from one another and from all other secondary schools in terms of location and clientele. But each was bound by these same constraints which bind the general run of secondary schools, and each embodies most of the changes in those schools that have stretched the organization to serve more people with more diverse educational programs. The task is to describe the pattern of activities that occurred in these three schools in order to understand how people behave in them, what activities are undertaken there, and what accommodations the inhabitants make to the constraints and to one another, and to use that description to develop a model of the structures of these three, and in some ways, of other secondary schools.

METHODOLOGY

The logic of the method should follow the logic of the question. Since the important unit of analysis is the structure, and the structure consists of behaviors and events, then it was imperative for me to get as close as possible to those behaviors and events. Hence I chose the field methods of participant observation and interview. I had had some experience with field methods when some years earlier, I attended school with some adolescent groups for the major part of their senior year.[6] That experience gave me sufficient understanding of the advantages and pitfalls of field methods, an understanding explained at length in the Appendix.

In the first study there was some limited participant observation with students, some black, some white, which gave me access to those situations in which the members of one race were either interacting with or reacting to members of the other race. It was a sensitive instance of participant observation because the topic was black–white interaction and our "whiteness" could have isolated us from black students. As it turned out, the black students had little trouble talking to us or having me and my colleague present during some of their very sensitive discussions. But it was made clear on some occasions that publicly affiliating with blacks did us no good with a number of whites whom we needed to fill out the other side of the story. Our solution in that study was to retreat from participant observation into a combination of observations and interviews. We found that while the school was a more lonely place than we would have liked, we had increased freedom to range about and contact more people about more events.

In the second study, I also tried to maintain a combination of participant observation and interview. When possible, I prefer participant observation. Personally, I know of no better way for an outsider to learn about an institution than to participate in its daily life and learn at first hand the perspective of the inhabitants. On a more practical level it makes one less of a stranger and hence relieves one from the problem of always having to explain one's presence. It gives one a place to go within the institution, some people with whom to associate, and most importantly, some intimates with whom to engage in a continuous and far-reaching dialogue, a dialogue in which sooner or later matters important to the study will be discussed. It is limiting, of course. If one joins with a few and if those few share some norms and expectations among themselves, then one must respect those norms and expectations even if it means limiting the contacts one would like to make with others. Nonetheless, the advantages outweigh the disadvantages. Participation on an intimate level gives one an access to the deeper life and the deeper meanings of the institution, so that even if one's contacts are more limited than one would like, and even if one has to rely more on inference to describe other parts of the setting, then those inferences have a greater reliability than can be had by sporadic contacts with many.

In the second study, I was much more successful maintaining a role of limited participant with some of the teachers, teachers who had the same kind of background and were roughly of the same age as I, while at the same time I was reasonably free to do as much observing and interviewing as I liked with people with whom I was less familiar.

While the methods, focus, and schools were all somewhat different across the studies, the basic structure of each school was very like that of the other two, and the methods (i.e., participation, observation, and interview) were also sufficiently similar so that in all three places I was engaging in the same activities (observing classes, interviewing teachers and students, taking a limited role in discussions, and pursuing issues of curriculum or public relations through the organization). The constant overlap in my activities was such that even in the third school, I was doing the same study I had done in the first school. Each study was begun from a different perspective, but each was at base a study of the structure of all three, and as I will argue, the general structure of secondary schools.

NOTES

1. P. Cusick and R. Ayling, "Biracial Interaction in an Urban Secondary School," *School Review*, 1974, *82*(3): 486–494.
2. P. Cusick, "A Study of Networks among Professional Staffs of Secondary Schools," *Educational Administration Quarterly*, 1981, *17*(3): 114–138.
3. For example, see C. A. Clinton, "The Politics of Developmental Change" (Washington, D.C.: National Institute of Education, Contract No. OEC-0-72-5245, 1977), p. 110; H. Wolcott, *Teacher vs. Technocrat* (Eugene: Center for Educational Policy and Management, University of Oregon, 1977); M. Q. Patton and V. Perrone, "Does Accountability Count without Teacher Support? An Assessment of the Kalamazoo Public School Account System from the Perspective of Teachers," Kalamazoo, Michigan, 1976; H. Bleecher, "The Authoritativeness of Michigan's Educational Accountability Program," unpublished dissertation, Michigan State University, 1975.

4. For example, see J. Meyer and B. Rowan, "The Structure of Educational Organization," in M. Meyer and associates, eds., *Environments and Organization* (San Francisco: Jossey-Bass, 1978), pp. 78–109; K. Weick, "Educational Organizations as Loosely Coupled Systems," *Administrative Science Quarterly*, 1976, *21*(3):1–19.
5. P. Cusick and W. Peters, "The Secondary Principal in the Small Town," *Secondary Education Today*, 1979, *20*(2): 22–36.
6. P. Cusick, *Inside High School* (New York: Holt, Rinehart and Winston, 1973).

2

Race, Discipline, and Attendance: The Basic Issues

INTRODUCTION

The basic pattern of American secondary education is fairly universal and fairly simple. The schools are large and diverse, and share a comprehensiveness which was designed, according to Conant, to "provide a general education for all future citizens, to provide good elective programs for those who wish to use their acquired skills immediately upon graduation [and] to provide satisfactory programs for those whose vocations depend on their subsequent education in a college or university."[1] To accomplish all of this, each secondary school has a principal, most (depending on size) one or more assistant principals, teachers specialized within subject areas, counselors, and secretaries to keep the paper work flowing and to account for the students. Each has a physical plant, more or less well equipped with corridors and classrooms, specialty areas, lockers, and offices. Each has a variety of courses, fewer for the smaller, more for the larger, schools offered at fixed intervals to batches of students, each of whom has some freedom to choose a set of courses appropriate to him or her. Among that set of courses are some that are required of everyone, usually English, government, and perhaps one or two years of science and math. Among the electives are whole ranges of additional courses, both from these areas mentioned and others such as vocational, home economics, music, career, cooperative, and physical education.

Course requirements are expressed in terms of credits. One has to have a certain number to graduate and those credits are measured in units of time spent on the subject. One year of algebra (one hour of class a day for the 180 days in the year) is worth one credit. One-half credit of government is given for one hour a day for the 90-day semester. Most four-year secondary schools expect a student to complete between 17 or 18 and 22 or 23 credits to earn the diploma, and following the goal of comprehensiveness, each school provides a number of paths toward the accumulation of the necessary credits. Even in a small school the courses are quite varied. The students are equally varied, coming from different groups and classes and having differing abilities, interests, and ambitions.

Since almost without exception, all public secondary schools, including those that were studied, adopted this general arrangement of people and facilities, it is not necessary to explain the particulars of the arrangement in the three schools. Rather I will enter quickly into the task of describing and explaining how people perform their roles, how they behave toward one another, and the way events unravel in those places. If in order to explain a certain event some explanation of the arrangements is necessary, that explanation will be added to the account. The overall emphasis here is not so much on the hierarchy and sequence of events in the schools as it is on the way that people behave within that hierarchy and sequence of events. It is these descriptions that will provide the clues to the structure.

These studies took place in a large industrial area in the northern United States. The name and location of the area are not important. It has the usual characteristics: an affluent inner city located on the site of the original harbor/trading post where today the financial and legal services, hotels, restaurants, and fine stores serve their clientele; a surrounding area characterized by decaying houses, abandoned hotels, vacant, rubbish-strewn lots and empty factories interspersed with older homes and decaying neighborhoods; a further ring of older suburbs, some with beautiful homes, shopping centers, hotels, and newer factories; and an even further ring of suburbs, some affluent, most designed for people in the middle-income ranges. The entire region covers a total of 1,500 square miles and the major part of six counties. Within that area lie some smaller industrial cities which are economically and socially and politically bound up with the central metropolis. Some of these are large enough to display many of the characteristics of the central metropolis. They too have a central area, many factories, affluent neighborhoods, and areas divided according to race. They too are an integral part of the metropolitan area. Of the schools described in this book, one is located in a far northern suburb populated entirely by whites, and two are in the centers of the smaller industrial cities.

The history of the area even to this day is one of growth, industrialization, and movement. Each of those elements is generated by and helps generate the other two. There always seems to be opportunities for some group of immigrants seeking to better its lot; the latest group is from the Arab lands in the Near East. Before that the southern United States sent first its blacks, then its whites into the area. Before that there were southern and eastern Europeans and even earlier, northern Europeans. The history of the area can be told in terms of movement by groups from one or another area of the country or the world, each trying to improve its lot at the same time the members stayed with "their kind." The schools all serve certain bounded districts and reflect the people who live within those districts. Whereas in former times, the schools reflected ethnic differences and to a very limited extent still do, today the primary division is by race.

The issue of race has dominated many of the area schools for years. Its effects have been felt all the way through the structure and the curriculum, and for that reason it merits some brief background. Two of the schools studied were large and biracial and each of those had a history of racial animosity. The northernmost school was composed entirely of whites, most of whom moved into the area in the previous twenty years, and many of whom moved out from the central city when they found the blacks moving into their neighborhoods and schools. This movement of whites from the inner to the outer areas was continuing well into the time of the study. Both inner schools had changed their population from predominantly white to predominantly black in the ten years previous to the study, and the movement continues at this writing.

Racial differences and the attendant conflicts and animosities have been the dominant issue in the area's schools for the fifteen years prior to the study. Before that time, there was some limited integration in the secondary schools but the elementary schools were almost completely segregated as were the neighborhoods. Until the advent of court-ordered busing, the black population had been confined in the poorer areas in the central city and by the rivers and behind the plants in the smaller cities. This de facto segregation in housing led to a corresponding segregation in the schools. While no one denied that segregation in schools was a fact, it was not then the issue it was to become. The boards of education throughout the area were genereally committed to neighborhood schools. This was explicitly stated in the district where the latter study took place.

> Pupil placement practices of the school district must be based on sound educational principles and should provide integrated school populations insofar as this is possible. The neighborhood school concept is believed to represent sound educational practice. Pupils will be guaranteed the right to attend the school which serves their attendance area as established by the action of the Board of Education.[2]

But even at the time of that statement, it was common knowledge that school segregation within districts that contained black students was to be attacked in the courts, and in fact the district where that statement was part of school board policy was the first of the metropolitan area's school district to be so challanged. The reasoning behind that challenge was that this smaller city had the same kind of industrial-base, social makeup, and segregation of blacks from whites as had the central metropolis. If it could be demonstrated that school desegregation worked in that smaller city, it could be argued that it would also work in the central metropolis.

In 1970 in that city a suit was filed by the state Civil Rights Commission stating that "Negro and Spanish American citizens had been excluded from

full participation in employment, housing, education, and social services
. . . [they] are denied equal protection under the laws and equal access to
jobs and law enforcement agencies . . . [they] are growing more and more
distrustful of a community they feel is trying to contain them." More specifically, the report of the Commission went on:

> De facto school segregation has existed since before World War II. This is
> true primarily because the city's educational program is organized on a neigh-
> borhood basis. Testimony given at the inquiry indicates that the racially seg-
> regated composition of the city's schools will continue until the neighborhoods
> become integrated or the school board takes affirmative action to achieve
> racial balance.[3]

This report by the Civil Rights Commission set the stage for a suit filed by
the NAACP, and as a result of that suit a federal judge found that the
nine new schools built in that district between 1955 and 1963 served to
strengthen segregation. He then ordered immediate integration of the district's schools and also the submission of a plan for their permanent and
complete integration. The district cooperated by submitting a plan to
integrate the segregated elementary and intermediate schools by busing,
which was implemented in 1971, and was met by a considerable and
sometimes violent reaction. Eventually the reaction and violence dimin-
ished, the buses rolled, the schools went on, but the whites accelerated
their exodus to the surrounding areas.

In the larger metropolis, the desegregation plans were proceeding with
an eye toward the events just described. Beginning in 1969, the Board of
Education, under pressure from the state Civil Rights Commission and the
threat of court action, adopted a desegregation plan for the city's secondary schools. This triggered a series of events beginning with the recall of
the four school board members who voted for the plan, and the actual
overturning of the plan by the state legislature and the governor. The
overturning was then reversed by a federal district judge who ordered a
desegregation plan which included not only the major metropolis but also
some white suburban school districts. The white districts that were to be
affected challenged that order and carried the challenge to the U.S.
Supreme Court, which approved of the city's desegregation plan but
refused to support cross district busing. According to the critics,
this ruling gave those who did not wish to integrate their chance to
escape to the suburbs, where the schools would remain just as white as the
residents. At that time it was argued by critics that the decision by the
Court allowing the white suburbs to escape desegregation destroyed the
intent of desegregation and assured that the city's schools would become
predominantly black. Whatever the reason, that is what happened. In 1974
the population of the major city's school district was 67 percent white; in
1982 it was 91 percent black.

BIRACIALISM IN THE SCHOOLS

While these events were taking place in the courts and legislatures, in the schools there was an increasing number of racial conflicts fomented by angry blacks who learned their militancy at home or on the streets, and resentful whites, who did not understand why they should be the recipients of the ill effect of three-hundred years of white injustice toward blacks. At the beginning of integration some school people we knew tried to smooth out these problems by addressing them directly in meetings with students. But it became quickly apparent that there was no rational way to deal effectively with this emotional issue. So those efforts were dropped, and instead the school people tried to play down or ignore the hostility, resentment, and anger and simply prevent or at least contain the resulting behavioral problems.

It was a very difficult time, and as I will explain, the events had some serious and lasting effects on the schools. The first study took place in 1972 in a school which will be referred to throughout this book as Urban High. Our orienting questions in that study were, What do black and white students do together in school? and How does what they do or do not do together affect other elements of the organization? While the study took place some years ago, an understanding of what happened in Urban High when the issue of racial relations was making headlines is essential to understanding the structure of the very similar biracial, urban school, Factory High, which we studied seven years later.

Urban High had a long history of black and white students being together. But at the time of the study the relations were deteriorating and in response, the administrators were beginning to make some changes in the organization. In fact the changes made at Urban High during the study and in the year following served as a model for all the biracial schools in the metropolitan area, including of course Factory High. Therefore I had the opportunity to witness the events that fomented the changes, the changes, and seven years later the effects of some of those changes.

Urban High was a 25 percent black, urban school with 1,900 students located in the center of a highly industrialized area. At the time of the study it was beset with an endless number of small and random but violent incidents, no one important by itself, but the sum of which dominated other events in the school. A description of some of these events can help explain the stresses and strains to which these biracial, urban schools were subjected.

"You see that play, *In White America*? No? Well, we had it last year and it was bad, all the niggers kept yelling, like anytime 'black' was mentioned, they'd yell and scream and yell and raise the fist, and when the word 'white' came up, they'd boo and holler. I was mad, I mean, I paid to see it and I was with my girl" (he was peering around the corner to see if some passing blacks were gone when he was talking) "and there's those guys in front of us . . ." (indicating the blacks who had passed) "Yeah, and finally she and I can't see, so I asked this guy to quiet down and he doesn't, so I get to kicking his seat and he turns around and says he's gonna kick my ass. 'Well,' I says, 'Okay, man, you wanna start it, go ahead,' but he doesn't do anything, just starts talking to his friends and mumbling but they quiet down . . . And the next day I'm in social studies and my girl comes in crying and tells me that him and his friends are bothering her, like, you know, they come up and act like they're going to hit her and then stop right in front of her face. So I go down and see that bastard and call him out, but he won't come, man, and then later I'm leaving and I see him down by the door and I call and say, 'You wanna get in it, man' and he's all alone, you know me and him, but then when he comes out following me there's six more of them step out. 'OK, man, I'll wait,' I says and later he saw me in class and gives me the sign and I just told him, 'F— you, nigger' . . ." Oooo, man, later they beat up my girl's brother in the locker room, stabbed him. Well, not stabbed really but slashed in the side."

It was not just talk of violence; there were numerous small incidents that attracted no attention and one had to look closely to even see. During a fire drill I went out the north door and was standing with a teacher. There were at least two hundred students around and one black boy said something to a smaller white boy. He then called the white over, took him by the arm and again said something to him, I couldn't tell what, but the smaller boy was saying, "What did I do?" . . . "Why pick on me?" The larger boy was backing him up holding his own arms out, snapping his fingers and humming, looking around to make sure no one was watching, and then—he hit the white two shots in the face, openhanded but hard. The white covered up and turned into his group of friends, none of whom gave any indication that their friend had just been hit. It looked as if the three blacks to whom the black boy then turned were the only ones who saw what had happened. The bell rang to return and I asked the teacher if he had seen it. "Where, where did that happen, who were they, do you remember?" I said I didn't know . . . Then he asked if I had seen much of that and I said a number of times. "Well, I've been here eighteen years and I never saw anything like that." Later, that same day, a group of black students were in the lavatory. One would come out, look around, and go back in. Two more would come out . . . "Send us a whitey—gonna kill him." A white student got up and went to the lavatory and when he came back, he had a growing welt over his right eye and his shirt was torn. "They were shoving me . . . wouldn't let me out . . . These f— niggers. I'm gonna go get me a .32, I'm tired of this s—." "Forget it," advised his friend. And forget it is what people did. Such random bits of occasional violence went on all the time and it seemed that even the participants took as little notice of them as possible.

Once in a mechanics class, when a car the students were working on was in the garage, a white student and another boy (also white) came into the auto shop and the teacher asked, "Where you been?" "I been thrown out. Here's my pink slip. See? Five days for fighting." I asked him what had happened and he explained: "I walked into the cafeteria and two niggers, one of them started giving me the shoulder. I pulled back. Then he kept giving me the shoulder and the other one started kicking me. I went ape s—, man. They were all around me, so my buddies couldn't get to me. This one dude kicking me, and the other punching me. I only got hit once that I felt, in the eye." Another boy said, "Who did it?" He said, "Two niggers. I don't remember what they looked like." "This will mean a lot of fights." "For everybody?" "No, just for me. After you fight one of those dudes they all want to fight you."

One should not get the impression that the school was riot-torn or that these isolated events disturbed the running of the school, nor that all fights were racial. There were as many fights involving black with black and white with white as there were involving black with white. And even when a fight between black and white did occur, there was no general talk by whites or blacks of "getting" those of the other race. The students who were involved intentionally or unintentionally were willing to ignore it and teachers seemed to choose not to see it. All were more than willing to let it pass off and go on about their individual business. In fact, even as the boy in auto shop was talking, there were three black students within hearing range and while they paid no overt attention to him, neither he nor his white listeners paid any attention to them.

The students had this interesting way of playing down the violence, even the bits of it in which they were personally involved. They had been in biracial situations for several years, at least since sixth grade, when they had begun attending centralized schools, and they had come to accept these incidents as part of the school scene. To them the biracial animosity and the violence that it occasioned did not deserve much comment. However, they did not ignore it completely. They knew where not to sit in in the cafeteria, whom to leave alone, which lavatory or stairwell or entrance to avoid, but it did not need talking about or getting excited over. Sometimes we would ask them about it: "It's just a f—up man, just a f— up." "No big deal, but you gotta be careful." "You should have seen it in junior high, fights all the time, it's better now." "What can you do?"

Even Herbie, a particularly militant black student, was unwilling to let an incident of fighting go too far. "You know down in that auto shop, that's where the Klan hangs out. I don't know if they're Klan, but that's the way those guys think." "But you've got Mr. F. [the teacher] in there, he's black." "Yeah, but he sticks his head under a car, he don't see nothin'. So, if he don't see it happen, he don't pay no attention to it. If he sees it happen, then he does something about it. I was down there and they had this white dude that F. appointed as assistant and this white dude was checking all the black guys, trying to throw them out of class, and they're after me because I shoot my mouth off a lot. They figure I'm the big mouth. They figure that if they can get to me, then they can get to all the brothers. I was running a welding unit, and someone turned the thing over, it was going to explode or something, you know. I yelled out for everyone to get out of the shop. Eighty-five guys walked out of the shop and this white guy got mad and hit me, threw me down. And then" (Herbie got excited) "and then I took a hacksaw to his ass, I took a hacksaw to the f—er's ass. I got thrown out of school, but that night there were two car-loads of guys up at my house, my relatives. They were going to come down and tear the place apart. But I said, 'No, I don't want to do that. I don't want to hurt Mr. F.' I told them that I'd go back and see. So I went back and saw the principal the next day, and that white dude was gone—they never saw him again. So I told my relatives to lay off. They called me chicken. But those guys—they shouldn't do that to Mr. F."

In truth, it was a stand-off bred of respect. The blacks I knew were hesitant to start a large-scale incident. They knew they were out-numbered, and they also regarded many whites with respect. As John explained, "They used to say that one black was worth two whites, but not any more. Some of those whites are really bad ass . . . I know this one white kid—last year he started something and about fifteen blacks were around . . . and he had a hold on one black kid and was going to kill him. It was going on in the library and I heard about it and I made it all the way from the cafeteria to the library in about two minutes. I was the only black up there who punched this kid. The other black kids, they were just standing around. After I hit him, he went down and then the others started, but they wouldn't be the first. And last year there were about seven white guys beating up one black kid . . . two of the kid's friends over there and one had a razor and they didn't do anything about it. The kid's girl friend came out and threatened them with a bottle and then they quit . . ."

A white agreed with John. I asked him if it were true that at one time any black could take two whites. "Yeah . . . it used to be that way, one black guy could, not any more, though. The white guys will swing right back. They know they can't get away with beating up white guys like that any more."

A casual visitor to the school would have seen little of what has been described. He would have seen halls empty of people except for the few minutes between each class, students grouped in their classrooms under the supervision of teachers, administrators and hall guards walking the halls, stopping one or another student and asking for a hall pass. But a close examination of the place revealed a large number of these small iso-lated incidents, any one of which in the opinion of the administrators might have triggered a general disruption in the student body. And it was that general disruption in the student body that the administrators worked so hard to avoid because it could have destroyed the appearance of safety and orderliness which the school had to present to the public. As the principal expressed it, "The important thing is safety. People have to know that if they send their children here, it's safe. That's what we work on, all the time." And so the efforts of the principal, deputy principal, administrative assistant and assistant principal for curriculum, and four hall guards were directed at maintaining constant surveillance of the halls, the lavatories, and the cafeteria in an effort not so much to prevent incidents of the type described (they were impossible to prevent), but to prevent them from spreading into the general student body. What could not be tolerated was a general student disruption accompanied by the TV cameras, police in the schools, and fearful parents (some of whom had a bad habit of carrying guns) coming to take their children home to safety. That had happened twice in the previous year, and from the administrator's point of view it was intolerable and the reason why the administrators were gradually changing the school. They were then in the process of eliminating the cafeteria periods, study halls, and activities, and locking certain lavatories. To a person, they felt they were dealing with a very dangerous situation. The prevailing attitude among them was, "Get them in, keep them busy, and get them out."

Another solution would have been to confront the issue of racial animosity directly, try to "deal with" it in the curriculum, and seek to ameliorate it through positive action rather than simply trying to keep the students apart. This was suggested by many, both within and without the school, and on some occasions I had the opportunity to witness events where whites and blacks, under the supervision of staff members, tried to deal reasonably with the issue.

April 4 was the anniversary of Martin Luther King's death, and as they had done in the previous year, some black students in the NAACP with Mr. L.'s direction were planning a program to honor black people. Herbie was among those who scoffed at it. "I don't do nothin' on Martin Luther King Day. They don't let us do nothin'. Like last year—we were going to appoint monitors and let them go around the halls and check kids' passes. We were going to have a Black Day when we could do our thing— a black holiday. Like you have Christmas and Easter, right? Thanksgiving? We were going to have Martin Luther King Day, do whatever we wanted to do. But last year when we had that day we were having a rap in the gym and the administrators came along and threw us out. They always do that."

But not always. The day was planned and Herbie was there, just as he said he would not be. There were a number of interesting events that day, one being a production of the play *Raisin in the Sun*, at which 700 of the 1,900 students were in attendance, 100 of them white and only 20 of them white boys. For the few whites, it was openly intimidating, with the majority blacks booing the lone white who appeared in the play as the landlord and applauding the black son who chased him out of the door. There were additional cries throughout the play of "black power" and "kill the whites." Following the play there was an "open discussion of race relations" which was to take place in the library. There were approximately 300 students in the library, only 24 of them white, and most of them girls. I noticed that they were among the well dressed and affluent looking. Two had tennis rackets.

Right away Mr. L. tried to start it off by calling on Mrs. O., a well-liked Chinese-Hawaiian teacher. She started by saying that she was disturbed because she thought it was Human Relations Day and there was only one race there. "Let's quit talking and start fighting," said the boy sitting next to me, the same one who had punched the student during the fire drill. At that point, Derrick and Carl got up: "Well, that's not the purpose of the day, to get whites and blacks together. Whites and blacks will never get together. The purpose of the day is to get blacks together. That's what we came to talk about. We came to talk about being black." Mrs. O. and the black hall guard who initiated the day got angry at that. They tried to point out that the title of the day was not Black Awareness, but Human Relations. Carl didn't agree. "Martin Luther King was a good nigger who got shot trying to be a good nigger. What's the sense in trying to be a good nigger with the whites? *What we want is more black awareness.*"

The teacher got more angry. "If you want me to go, then, I'll leave. If the purpose of this day is black awareness, I'm not black, so I'll leave." Derrick said, "*Go ahead, we ain't stopping you.*" Then Herbie got up and said, "I came to talk about blackness. If the purpose of this day is just to talk about human relations, I gotta go get a haircut." He put on his hat and walked out, amid howling and yelling. There were only a few blacks—Herbie, Derrick, Tony, and Carl—who were vocally favoring a black awareness session, but they clearly had the crowd with them. Steve was talking about making a revolution. "Let's do something." Barbara, as student council president, was trying to get a dialogue going with the teacher, but it was simply impossible to start a dialogue with anyone when Carl, Derrick, Herbie, and Tony—all of whom were sharp witted, articulate, and militant—kept harrassing her. Mr. L. got very upset and said that what he was trying to do was "make it Human Relations Day not just Black Awareness Day." He was trying to shut the boys up but they were calling him "Tom," and "Mr. Jones."

But he tried: "The NAACP started the day, we started it to try and talk about it, and now you come up here and try to turn it into something else. You're tearing it apart." Derrick would not take that. "Mr. D., [the black deputy principal] didn't you make me come in this library? Now you made me come in," (Mr. D. nodded) "I'm going to make it what I want. If this is Human Relations Day, *Where are the whites?*" Derrick was right, of course, very few whites were even in school that day, and there were only six or seven in the library. (The rest of the twenty-four had left.)

When Derrick said, "Where are the whites," one white girl raised her hand. "I want the blacks to stop talking about being black all the time and get to trying to get along with some whites." As soon as she said that, everybody went "booooo," but she went on. "If the blacks withdraw from society, they'll just be cutting themselves off, and if you cut yourself off from whites, as you're doing, then you'll never get back in." At this a lot of them hollered, "Yeah, who wants to get back in?"

That was a good example of what happened when the issue of race was treated openly and some attempt was made within the curriculum to treat it in a reasonable fashion to ameliorate tensions between blacks and whites. The blacks brought in their militancy, which dominated all of the black discussions even though many black students did not have those feelings. The whites stayed out of school, or if in school, stayed out of the events. One could understand the behavior of the administrators who had witnessed such events time and again and tried only to contain the problems rather than trying to treat them directly.

At one point, later in the afternoon, an organizer from the NAACP came in to give a speech to the students, and went on to suggest some possible solutions to racial problems. At the end of his talk, one white girl wanted to extend the possible solutions into the school and asked, "But what can we do to get together?" Barbara, the black president of the student council, said quietly, "Nothing, there's nothing you can do. Don't even try."

What I saw in that school was that while the regular curriculum with the classes, tests, activities groups, and informal friendships continued as in any secondary school, there was a constant undercurrent of racial animosity which manifested itself in numerous ways each day and which was always capable of surfacing to foment a serious incident. Certainly there was a strong element of hard-core racism on the part of many whites. That racism was countered by an angry and articulate group of blacks who were constantly looking for a chance to turn anything into an incident. While I believe that they were in a minority among the blacks, their voices always dominated the black discussions. For them, there was only one issue worth studying in the school and that was white oppression of blacks, and given the opportunity they would turn any discussion to that end. One of the events I attended regularly was the discussion days in the black studies classes. Though a former teacher in urban schools, I was still ignorant of the feelings of the black students, and I always felt it was a privilege to attend these discussions by black adolescents about the problems of being black in a white world. On occasion there were angry words exchanged among them on how to accommodate the white institution. During one discussion the question became, "Why can't black basketball players give the sign?" This was a month-old issue involving a racial incident at a basketball game. A black Urban High player had threatened an opposing white player and the blacks had been particularly incensed because, while the Urban High player was blamed, it was claimed that the white player had called him a nigger. Following the incident there was a ruling from the central office which said among other things that black players were not to raise their fists during the national anthem. The basketball players stopped giving the "sign" and continued playing, which further angered the militants. Herbie's point was: "The white man takes off his hat or holds his hand over his heart, right? Well, why can't we salute our way?" (I was frankly surprised at that, never having considered the power sign as a means of saluting the stars and stripes.)

Then they began to berate Henry, a basketball player, who gave up giving the power sign in order to continue playing. Herbie, Frank, and Dan said he should have stopped playing basketball, which was "just a white man's game." Some girls defended him: "Well, Henry does it because that's the way he can get a college scholarship." Frank didn't like that: "There are lots of ways to go to college without having to sell out the brothers and sisters to get there." A lot of girls felt that "Henry had the right to play ball if he wanted to. It was his game and he wanted to play it." Mr. B. thought so too. But Herbie, Frank, and Derrick were unanimous. "Henry shouldn't play on the team; to do so is simply disloyal to the cause. Since everything is white, we should separate ourselves as much as possible and the black basketball players are not doing it."

By the time the class ended, Frank in particular was all worked up and went out the door looking for an incident. I headed for the third-floor library to write it all down, but something was going on in the halls. There was a group of blacks, Frank in the center, down at the end of the third-floor hall. Black students were going toward that end and whites were heading the other way. There were a lot of calls of "Black Power" and "Right on!" One locker was open and then I saw that about fifteen blacks had a short, overweight, white student in the middle. One hit him, knocked something out of his hand, and he was roughly pushed against the locker. When he bent down to pick up his book, Frank kneed him in the left side. Someone else hit him before they let him go and he came down the hall past me, tears in his eyes. The Spanish teacher, who was white, was then in the middle telling them to leave, but they were surrounding him. Frank walked around behind, raised his hand over the teacher's head, and pointed down, as if to say "Get him." But they didn't do it. They saw the hall guard and the deputy principal coming down the hall and broke up.

Frank was escorted to the office while the others who were involved simply left. Nothing came of it in the form of suspension or expulsion. It was just passed off as another random bit of violence and Frank was in school the next day.

The administrators could have expelled him if they wanted to, but punishing Frank was not their major goal nor was it in their best interests. Any move like that would have been regarded as "racist" by a large number of blacks and could have caused additional trouble. And, too, a number of teachers considered Frank intelligent and sensitive and, when he wanted to be, a very personable individual. When he did cause trouble it was likely to be passed over.

We began the study asking what blacks and whites did together and what their mutual patterns of interaction or noninteraction did to other aspects of the school. We wanted to have some clearer idea of what kind of effects biracialism combined with strong animosity placed on the school. While I have yet to explain some of the effects of that element on classrooms and on teachers, there are some general answers. The blacks and whites did very little with one another in the school, and their mutual suspicion and distrust was the basis of a larger number of racially motivated incidents than anyone was willing to admit. Blacks and whites were never together in the corridors, in the cafeteria, or in the classrooms. There was little sharing of informal conversations, and there was pressure on the blacks by other blacks to avoid school-sponsored activities that were predominantly white. There was resistance from blacks to other blacks who would have liked more interaction with whites, and there was open intimidation of whites who were with blacks of the opposite sex. One time after I had been talking in the halls to a black girl with whom I used to check certain events, I was pointedly asked by five black boys if I was "seeing that young lady."

In Chapter 1 I outlined some of the general constraints on the structure of secondary schools, for example, funding patterns and the requirement that they take and provide some instruction for everyone. The constraint that was most evident in this school and the equally biracial Factory High was that so much organizational energy had to be invested in suppressing numerous racial incidents, any one of which could have spread into a general disruption and destroyed whatever orderliness the school contained and whatever faith the people of the community had in the school. Overall, Urban High was an orderly and well-run place, but only because so much organizational effort was directed to that end. Our conclusion about biracialism was that it was the most powerful of any of the factors operating in the school because of the potential it had for disruption and violence. This potential dominated everything in the school.

Any organization has a number of basic elements. There is a formal structure with roles, patterns of communication and activity, an authority structure, a technology or some means of applying resources to raw material, and some agreed-upon goals. Perhaps most important, there is a general awareness on the part of the participants of what the organization is all about, as well as a sense of knowing when it has or has not accomplished its task. In addition there is the factor of "consensual basis" or a sense of "mutual cooperation" among the members. While this school had the formal structure and the belief by the participants in the worthwhileness of the endeavor, there was no consensual basis or sense of mutual cooperation among the students.

Even aside from race, the potential for conflict among students was obvious. They came from a wide range of cultural, social, and economic classes. Not only were the blacks and whites separated by language, customs, and color, but neither the blacks nor the whites were together among themselves. The blacks disparaged both those whom they called "rich kikes" and the boys in the auto shop, whom they called "white trash." Some of those called "rich kikes" also referred to the boys in the auto shop as "white trash." The boys in the auto shop talked of the "niggers and spades" while they, along with other whites, were referred to as "honkies" by militant blacks, who reserve a special hatred for those whom they call the "colored," the "toms," and the "white girl lovers." Moderate blacks refer to militants as "back bitin' muther—" and most of the students scorned the drug users. Cathy blamed the administration for keeping students suppressed, yet admitted that if they cooperated with the administration by exposing the pushers she might get hurt and she and her friends "didn't want to get involved."

The students in that school had so little in common with one another that none of them seemed to want to get involved, nor did there seem to be anything with which they could get involved. There was really no reason for students to have any consensual basis, communal spirit, or mutual cooperation. The various individuals and factions did not even like each other, and while they did not openly riot, and fights while frequent remained isolated, the reason they remained isolated was that the formal organization was structured to "keep the lid on."

This was the main point about biracialism and the organization of that high school. Biracialism was the strongest contributor to the creation of conflicts among the students and simultaneously it prevented the students from creating an adequate "consensual basis" which might have been used to resolve those conflicts. The response of the administrators to potential racial trouble was to structure the organization to prevent the numerous conflicts from disrupting the normal activities. Subsequently a number of decidedly restrictive characteristics were being considered at the time of the study and were implemented the following year. Periods were kept to 57 minutes with only a few minutes for passing. There were no free periods, study halls, or activity periods. The cafeteria serving time was brief the year of this study and all cafeteria service was eliminated thereafter. The administrators admitted they eliminated it for security reasons. School functions such as dances and parties were rare and later eliminated. Funds were allocated for four security guards and almost all of the administrator's time was spent on discipline. As the principal put it, "If there's any question, I find it best to say 'no.'" There was just no room for relaxation or experimentation. The total organization was gearing up to prevent the potential conflict among students from developing into violence. "Keeping the lid on" devoured all the excess energy that might have been used for pursuing other ends. Biracialism was not merely another element that had to be considered. It dominated everything else in the school.

Whether the organization even had the ability to begin conflict resolution is questionable because there was such a high degree of what Cosar refers to as "non-realistic conflicts," which, as he explains, "are not occasioned by rival ends of the antagonists, but by the need for tension release of one or both of them . . . insofar as it affords only tension release the chosen antagonist can be substituted for any other suitable target."[4] Frank led the group to the third floor not to settle a dispute with particular people but to express his outrage at white society's treatment of blacks. The white boy whom he assaulted did him no harm, he was just there and vulnerable. All the incidents I witnessed were just as random and isolated, and as far as the organization goes, just as "nonrealistic," that is, they were organizationally unresolvable. Perhaps it was most evident on Human Relations Day, when the well-intentioned girl asked, "But what can we do?" and Barbara told her, "Nothing . . . there's just nothing . . . don't even try." There is a looping effect at work here: The heavy emphasis on maintenance, or on keeping the students moving and getting them out before they had time to get into trouble, also reinforced biracialism. The students seldom had time to do other than go to class and do their work. They did little together to alleviate the potential conflict. This reinforced the biracialism that kept them apart.

The incidents recounted in the past few pages took place during the early 1970s, during the time of the greatest white flight from the inner cities, the time of the most outspoken black militancy, and during the time that both Urban High and Factory High were changing from a white majority to a black majority. There is the possibility that the problems that occurred then no longer occur. Even at that time, while the schools were approximately 65 percent white, there were as many white students involved in discipline and attendance cases, relative to their number, as there were blacks relative to theirs. And at least one of the administrators, a ninth-grade principal, maintained that the problems of race were somewhat exaggerated. "Everyone thinks that the problems here are racial, but they aren't, they're drug related. Someone is pushing in on someone else's territory and the fights start." That man in particular was having his problems, not so much with racial trouble as with the special education students, 140 of them in the ninth grade who were being mainstreamed into the regular classrooms at the demand of the state legislature. They caused him the most trouble, with their skipping, tardiness, and the general disruption they were causing in classes that they did not like or could not understand. And too, when those incidents described took place, the black students were in the process of "taking over" the school from the whites, who up to that time had dominated almost everything in the school. Since then in both schools the blacks have become the majority, and according to the administrators, no longer feel the need to be so assertive. As the whites left, the incidents of black-white conflict were severely reduced.

But the thesis that biracialism and the effects of biracialism exert a continuing and very strong influence on the structure of those schools is not dependent merely on the number of conflicts between black students and white students. The school I studied seven years later and most of the biracial schools in the metropolitan area, faced with the same types of problems as described here, also adopted the same administrative structure to deal with those problems. There were five periods each day, five days a week. There were no study halls or activity or free periods, no cafeteria, and few activities other than sports. The students came in at 7:30, had their five periods, and left at 12:40. After that the school was emptied of students save for a few participating in sports or activities. The thesis, that biracialism had some serious effects on the structure, is not dependent on the number of racial incidents as much as it is on the changes wrought as a result of the incidents, changes which persist to this day.

Also, racial animosity in schools is not a thing of the past. In Factory High in 1979, where there were more blacks than whites, there were fewer individual incidents, but there were still more racial incidents than were even admitted. There was still the separateness of whites from blacks in the classrooms and in the corridors, still the assaults, still the tension created by nonstudents in the parking lots and in the school if they could get in, and still the potential for trouble in classes between black students and white teachers. There was still the wariness in the community about reputed trouble in the schools. The economic conditions for blacks in the community outside the school had actually worsened between the time of the first and the time of the second study. The newspapers forgot about black bitterness toward the system, but the blacks did not forget it, and in Factory High, the worst thing that could occur and which the administrator worked constantly to avoid was general racial trouble which they had all experienced many times before. The problems seemed to occur less often than before, but they were still a real danger as evidenced by the precautions taken to prevent them, precautions that were developed as the staffs learned better how to guard against racial problems. Animosity between blacks and whites did not begin in 1967 and end in 1975. It was then that it received wide press coverage. But feelings of suspicion, distrust, and apartness persist to this day in those schools, as anyone who takes the time to watch the students in the corridors and classrooms can see. Along with the continued presence of the potential for racial trouble is the persistence of the structural elements that were developed to respond to it: the limited schedule, the police officers, hall guards, the five-by-five instructional day, and the behavior of the administrators, who devote most of their efforts to "keeping the lid on."

While racial animosity and its potential for general disruption were serious problems in two of the schools I studied, they were only part of a larger issue generally referred to as "attendance and discipline." In fact, they had the same generalized effects throughout the school as do those elements, that is the devouring of whatever administrative and supervisory resources are available, as well as some secondary effects which will be explained. What occurred in both Urban High in 1972 and Factory High in 1979 was that biracialism caused a great many problems, but biracialism per se was never addressed. Rather it was treated as a compounding element in the issue of maintaining order. The administrators felt there was no direct way to address race as an issue. The principal of Factory High put it clearly one day when, at a teachers' meeting, a black teacher suggested that most of the school problems could be traced to race. "We can't talk about that; there's nothing we can do about it and talking just doesn't do any good," was his answer. So the problems brought on by biracialism became problems of order, or more specifically problems of attendance and discipline, and were treated just that way.

DISCIPLINE AND ATTENDANCE

The task of secondary schools is not really simple, but it can be stated simply: To extend the offer of education to as many people as possible regardless of their background, ambitions, or abilities.

At base, the public schools are bound by the egalitarian ideal. As a nation we retain the hope that our citizens will have some fairly even chance at social, economic, and political equality. Since education is one of the most important ways to attain that equality, all children are obligated to come to school and similarly, the schools are obligated to appeal to all their students. Schools, then, are charged with providing some sort of educational experience for every child in the community, even those who may not be particularly interested in what is generally called "their education," or put another way, not particularly interested in the acquisition of positive knowledge. By positive knowledge I mean that which is generally accepted as having an empirical or traditional base, which is deemed socially useful, and which lends itself to expression in a verbalized and abstracted form. The assumption that the acquisition of positive knowledge can be made interesting and appealing in part underlies the laws that compel everyone to attend school, at least until their mid teens, and a corresponding requirement for the schools that they offer a sufficiently diversified curriculum to have some way to appeal to more varied constituents. The history of secondary schools for at least the last quarter century has been the continual fragmentation and diversification of the curriculum to appeal to the increased numbers of people coming to schools, people of a type who for one reason or another may not have come to school previously. While in this democratic and fluid society this assumption about the acquisition of positive knowledge is useful and appealing, it does seem that there are large numbers of people for whom the desire to learn does not come easily. One has to choose to be a serious learner. Many children who attend school never do make that choice. They go to school only grudgingly and while there remain continually unimpressed by the blandishments put forth by the staff. It is no secret that the urban biracial schools seem to have more of these students than one might expect than if such students were randomly distributed across the population.

The general behavior at Urban High and Factory High is quite good. These schools which had reputations for being "tough" places, did have some "tough" students, but students for the most part were decent and civil. Almost uniformly all have some interest in school: one or another class that they liked, a teacher with whom they shared a personal relation, some friends or interesting activities. But while such elements make school an appealing place to be, they are not sufficient to interest all the students in acquiring positive knowledge. Hence it was not surprising that many students became bored, perhaps insolent, or ran afoul of the rules and regulations. Such things happen in any school, but in the urban schools the number of such incidents is higher, because the number of students who tend to have school problems is higher. The effect is similar to the effects or the threat of racial trouble. Because of the resources allocated toward containing it, it tends to dominate other elements in the school.

It would be cheaper and simpler to throw the disorderly out. But the public schools base their claim to legitimacy on being able to appeal to all to assure that all receive their chance at equality. To simply throw out the disorderly and uninterested would be a public admission that there are a sizable number for whom the egalitarian ideal does not hold. But if it does not hold for some, then it does not hold at all. And if it does not hold, the public schools as we know them have no claim to legitimacy. A truant or disorderly student is an inconvenience, but a large number of truant or disorderly students is a threat to the legitimacy of the institution. That is why the schools have to devote whatever time and energy it takes to getting the reluctant to come to school and keeping them in a state of order once they are there.

Of course, in the schools where attendance and discipline are more problematic, even more energy has to be allocated in that direction. I was particularly interested in how these matters were handled in Urban High and in Factory High, both of which enjoyed a reputation for being "tough." Mr. D. was an administrative assistant in charge of discipline in Urban High:

> What a day . . . we started out with 20 dogs in the building this morning. We chased them all over the building but when we got back to the office, there

were 25 kids waiting. Halfway through them the junior high school called and they had food poisoning and dismissed 600 kids and 300 of them came over here. I'm running around all morning trying to get them out . . . How long can this last? I wonder what it would be like not to have to take all this crap every day.

But he believed in his role as an enforcer, and he believed that by enforcing he was teaching the students the basic lesson they had to learn.

You know what is the biggest problem we have here? . . . It's attendance. We can't get the kids to school and if we do we then have to get them to class. You really have to believe that what you're doing is right. I couldn't do it otherwise. Like . . . you know, what's the worst things kids can do, not knifing, not talking back to teachers, but skipping, because one thing we can't do is let kids come to class, walk in, look around and decide, "Well, I don't want to be here, I think I'll go home." Some day those kids will be in places where they have to show up and we have to teach them that.

What Mr. D. expressed was felt by all of the administrators whom we knew. The worst problem they had was getting students into the school and into classes where they would take the instruction seriously. If they could do that, then discipline problems would be lessened. Fewer problems arose when the students were in classes with teachers than when the students were not in classes. It was then that they would get into some situation which led them into the disciplinarian's office.

We noted that in some of the inner city schools in the larger metropolis, the principals reported a 15 percent absenteeism rate for Tuesday, Wednesday, and Thursday, but a 25 percent rate on Monday and Friday. In the area school reported to be the "roughest" in the inner city, the principal reported a 42 percent average absentee rate. In our urban schools it averaged 17 percent a day, in a further suburban school, 7 percent. In some of the rural schools the principals report a 4–5 percent rate. But in every secondary school studied, the administrators put a great part of their effort into maintaining attendance and discipline. In the urban schools where there was a higher absentee rate, more administrators were allocated to that task. In the suburban schools, which were smaller and better attended, it was still their dominant activity.

There are two levels to this problem. The first is getting the students to come to school, the second and even more difficult is getting them into class. In the school reported to be the "roughest" in the central metropolis, the principal reported a 90 percent attendance at school, 60 percent attendance at class. While the rate was lower in the schools we studied, it was that group who were in the building but not in class that caused the most trouble. They were the ones who were in the halls and lavatories, and the parking lots, who fomented the fights and assaults, and who showed up at the end of the year with a zero grade point average.

A look at the discipline record in the first urban school for the first six months of that year indicated the problems with attendance and discipline.

In Urban High, of the 1,900 students in the school at the year's beginning, 173 or 9 percent had dropped out by January, and another 410 students had been suspended for one or two days, the most frequent violation being "skipping class." The second most common violation was smoking, and that took place when students skipped classes. Together those offenses accounted for 374 of the 410 suspensions. The rest of the suspensions were for more serious offenses—fighting, carrying weapons, or intimidating a teacher or student. They too were violations that would not have occurred if the offenders had been in class doing what they were told by the teacher. Given that, one can understand Mr. D.'s perspective on what he claimed was at the root of all the problems of the school, individuals skipping class. Speaking once of a boy who was particularly troublesome:

> We missed the boat with him . . . he's a nice kid . . . personable but we should have got to him when he started skipping gym. Then we wouldn't be having the problems we're having with him now. We let him go and now he doesn't do anything. Not anything in school and not anything so bad that we can throw him out. Well, I came close to calling the police on him one day. But we should have kept after him. It wouldn't have been easy, but little by little he would have come around and now in his senior year he could be getting himself straight.

To better understand the perspective of Mr. D. one had only to spend some time in the offices of the assistant or associate principal, house or grade principal, or administrative assistant for attendance and discipline. In all of the schools, these offices consisted of large bays or anterooms dominated by a reception counter behind which a secretary (sometimes two) and perhaps some student aides worked. Off to the right or left, there were smaller offices for the administrators, a nurse, or an activities director. These anterooms were the scene of coming and going, of teachers coming in to check their mailboxes in the morning and in the evening, of people waiting to purchase tickets or get information about events, in one school to purchase snacks between classes, of attendance people and hall guards coming in to talk, drink coffee, exchange or obtain information; and in all the schools, these anterooms served as gathering places for the few teachers who were close friends of that particular administrator. There they would gather to talk and smoke, drink coffee, and carry on informally. Parents called for a conference or seeking some information would be in and out also.

But their main function was to serve the endless stream of students sent in to get a late admit slip, or an early release slip, a parking permit, a work permit, or a physical check permit, or who were there because they had been involved in some sort of disagreement with a teacher and were "sent to the office" or "called to the office." In no school was there a time when there were not at least three or four of these students in each office for tardiness, fighting, insolence, failure to come to or leave class as requested, failure to complete assignments, or whatever. Of all the reasons why students were there, most involved a dispute. They would explain the problem to the administrator, who, depending on the nature of the offense, would then send the student back to class with a note, arrange a meeting between the teacher and the student, keep the student until the end of the period, suspend him or her for a day, call the parent, or if the matter were serious, move into formal hearing processes. This round of visits or "problems" literally took up almost the entire day of these administrators. It took patience to deal with these issues:

"I didn't do nothing."

"Well, it says here you failed to hand in your work for five days in a row."

"That old teacher just didn't like me. Like all I do is walk in and she starts yelling."

"Did you do your homework?"

"Well, it wasn't my fault, my brother took my books."

The vice principal took out the contract that the student and he had signed, a contract by which the student agreed to do his homework and stating that he understood what would happen if he didn't do his homework, that he would fail his classes.

"You better start doing your work; if you don't, you'll fail and anyway, in two months you'll be sixteen and then we don't have to keep you here anymore."

The student agreed to do better, or at least acquiesced, said he would do his homework and try to get along with the teacher, and then sat out the period in the office before going to the next class. This was just another in an endless series of discrete events, each one handled separately, none related to the others, except in the general sense of sharing some characteristics. They were almost always minor, involving one teacher and one or two students. The students knew that they had transgressed but they did not seem very upset about it. Indeed, it was a small percentage who become involved in the great number of these incidents, and each time the perpetrator had a predictable excuse which was delivered almost ritualistically: "I forgot . . . my mother didn't wake me before she left . . . I didn't understand the assignment . . . he pushed me first . . . the teacher doesn't like me . . . I wasn't doing it, it was someone else . . . I didn't mean to hit him . . . she looked at me . . . nobody told me about it."

An interesting point about this round of events is that while administrators are fond of using "battle" metaphors to describe their discipline role, for example, portraying themselves as being "on the firing line," "in the trenches," "getting shot at," and so forth, this matter of student discipline seems to have little about it that is actually that "difficult." The problematic and difficult element is not so much the behavior that the student is engaged in or refusing to engage in as it is the emotional overtones accompanying that behavior. These overtones are most likely to emerge in the classrooms, where the teacher is trying to get the student to stop doing something or to do something he does not wish to do. There the emotions emerge and the teacher is most likely to receive the disrespect and abuse which become the problem. By the time the events gets down the hall or down the stairs to the administrator's office, the spectators are gone, emotions calmed, and the administrator not personally threatened. The whole thing is reduced to a procedure and a process, the main features of which are its repetitiveness and tiresomeness.

Among themselves, administrators were fond of speaking of their endless "problems," but it seemed to me that more often it was the teachers who handled the problems. After all, it is the teachers who are trying to change the student by pushing him somewhere he may not want to go, or asking him to become something he is not. Administrators most often ask only that he or she be orderly while not doing very much of anything. It is in the classrooms with from twenty to thirty students, each of whom the teacher has to be considering, that one or another of them may feel slighted, insulted, or wronged and may react with some words or actions that foment an incident. It is true that administrators may encounter the negative emotions and take the accompanying abuse when they interact with recalcitrant students, but the chances of that happening in their offices is less than the chances of it happening in the classrooms.

The administrators dealt with one student at a time, and rarely were students disorderly or disrespectful when they were with one person, or when they had the entire attention of that one adult. Also, when the incident reached the vice principal's office, other elements emerged. The student probably wanted to stay in school and he knew that if he continued his behavior with the administrator, he would be out. The administrators might very well have a good personal relationship with the students. Indeed, some of the worst-behaving students had their best relations with the school's disciplinarian. So, when the administrator made some judgment as to which of the procedures would be invoked, the parent called or the student suspended, removal from the particular class, or simply a warning not to do it again, students most often acquiesced and the whole thing drifted off into the record. By the time it reached the administrator, there was usually little left of the matter.

This was also true of the potentially more difficult issues, such as a fight between two boys, one black and one white, who were still mouthing threats when they reached the office:

"Hey, this dude thinks he's tough, and he wanted to start something . . ."

"You asked for it, you were picking on that little kid last week."

"That was none of your business and you didn't start nothing then."

"Well, I'll start something now . . ."

"Well, go ahead . . ."

But neither moved from the chair he was in. Nor did the vice principal, who knew it was all talk. The fight was over and both agreed to go home, accept the automatic suspension, and have their parents come to get them reinstated.

Attendance and discipline are major concerns in any school, particularly in our biracial urban schools with reputations for being tough. But the issue seemed not so much a problem as a pervasive fact of life, a fact which had been recognized long ago and to which considerable energy had been allocated to resolving or at least containing, removing its uncertainty and changing it from a problem to a procedure. And in each school I studied the administrators had done that quite successfully. Each school had its procedures and processes. Each had an adequate number of experienced administrators to implement the processes, and in Urban High, even with 410 suspensions and 173 dropouts a term, the school went on quite smoothly, because enough of its resources had been allocated to turn what could have been problems into procedures. There is little about these standard cases which occur over and over again that is really "problematic" as far as the organization goes.

The possible solutions to any particular issue were quite limited. They included only suspension or in some more serious cases expulsion, closing particular classes to the student, reprimands, a call to a parent with perhaps an accompanying conference with the parent and teacher. But the administrators' primary tool for use in these instances was an appeal, implicit or explicit, to the student to consider what he was doing to himself and his chances for an education, and the standard secondary appeal to consider his or her future in the outside world, when someone would demand to know about his school record. Almost all students accepted this line of thinking. Sometimes the administrator added a personal appeal based on the decent relationship that he had with the student. But rarely did it become emotional. Indeed, if an administrator allowed himself to become continually upset, he could probably no longer function.

An interesting feature about this issue was the idiosyncratic way it was handled by the administrators. What happened to a student sent to the administrator's office depended on the particular administrator. Teachers were quick to note the differences between administrators who "backed them up" and took some action and those who failed to do so, and they were particularly disparaging of those who in their view did nothing or simply sent the student back to the class. They continually disparaged one administrator who would suspend a student for some offense pending a parent conference, but if the student, right there in the office, called the parent and had the parent talk to the administrator, the suspension was lifted. They ridiculed another who had reputedly told a student, "Now, John, you know you did it, you know you did, you assaulted that teacher, you have no excuse. Now when you return to school on Monday morning . . ." Nor did they appreciate a particular administrator whose office served as a social gathering place for a set of his friends and who, while the friends were there talking sports or money or gossiping, would go on lecturing students. They also disliked an administrator who would process some transgression by sending the student to another section of the same class without ever notifying either teacher, in effect writing the issue off as a personality conflict between the teacher and the student rather than treating it as a serious matter. They least appreciated the occasions where they suspected the administrator of siding with the student, of agreeing with the student that the teacher was wrong in that instance, and of striking an agreement with the student to go through the motions of taking action while doing nothing.

On the other hand, they appreciated the administrators who gave the students the clear idea that if they are sent to the office, "something will happen" to them. They liked the one who had her procedures all laid out; "They have to know that if they do this, this happens, if they do that, that happens, if this happens that follows, that's the only way to do it." Or the ones who demanded that the parents actually come to school for the conference, and made a point of following up on a referral even if it meant going out to find the student in the halls, or calling the parent at night from home.

It is not surprising that individual administrators in the same school had different ways of dealing with student issues depending on their own predilections. The requirement of public school is not so much that procedure and policies are followed as it is that a decent and orderly atmosphere be maintained. And if a particular administrator felt he or she could maintain the decent, orderly atmosphere using his particular style, then it did not matter too much what management procedures he or she used.

Criticisms of administrators we heard from teachers seemed to be divided into two sets. The first set consisted of expressions that one or another of the administrators was not following up or supporting them in particular instances. But another type of criticism came from teachers who felt that in general the administrators were setting the wrong tone for the school. "When I first came here a few years ago, I raised my hand in the first faculty meeting and asked why the ninth graders were coming in from the smoking area late for the first hour and I wanted to know why they had a smoking area, and I was told that they smoke anyway and they might as well have a smoking room, and I knew what to expect in that school, I knew right there . . . they set too much emphasis on the police function, they don't set the tone, there isn't enough getting the kids to respect the place and respect themselves, we make the place a prison and the kids treat it like a prison." What that teacher wanted was not so much help with a particular child (indeed, her relations with her students were known to be good), but she wanted the administrators to be strong and respected. If they were, then there would be fewer occasions on which they would have to send students out, because the students would behave in such a way as to avoid being sent out.

In Factory High School, in particular, this was a commonly discussed issue, but it was true in Suburban High also. As many teachers saw it, strong and consistent administrators could reduce their in-class problems.

What they saw were too many administrators who were inconsistent, overly personal with students, unable to implement the discipline policies as written and therefore unable to provide them the help they felt they needed. As one teacher recounted: "This girl had been in and out of class, and in and out of trouble, and I told her one time to get out and go see the administrator, and in front of the whole class she says, 'I can get around any administrator in this school any time I want,' and I told her to go do it, and sure enough she was back a few minutes later and announced to the class that the administrator had told her to go back to class, just what she said she would do. 'Out,' I told her, 'out,' and right there she said: "F— you, f— this class, and f— this whole place"; and she left.

According to that teacher, had the girl known there was some authority to be reckoned with in that school, then she would not have behaved that way in the first place. In fact, there was one administrator in the school whom that particular girl admitted she could not get around. According to her "he's a bitch," but according to the teachers he was the best of the group. During that same conversation they brought up the story of one of the administrators who, being told by the art teacher that a student's behavior was just terrible, removed that student from the class. But a few days later, the woods teacher came to the art teacher and asked if it were true, as the administrator had told him, that if he kept that boy in woods, the boy could have credit for art. The teachers thought that was just terrible, although a good example of the kind of accommodations that administrators made with students. Speaking again of the girl who told the teacher what he thought of him and everything else, he said, "I don't know what happened to her, but I'm going to find out. She has to have the credit to graduate and I'm not going to have that mark changed. I'll go to the post on this one."

In fairness to what is being presented as the teacher's views, the administrators in all the schools did have different ways, of interacting with students and of administering the codes. In Chapter 3, I will explain the very different ways teachers have of approaching their classes and interacting with students, ways which emanate from their personalities. Similarly, the administrators had had successful careers as teachers as evidenced by their promotion to administrative positions. But that promotion was based largely on their ability to get along with and hence control the behavior of students, particularly the more difficult. Many of them did this by maintaining good personal relations with students; when they become administrators, they retained their concern about good personal relations and put the maintaining of those relations before the policies and procedures. In the schools I studied, for most administrators, maintaining good personal relations was more important than adhering to policies and procedures.

Teachers might not like the man who allowed the students to be reinstated before they even left the building, but the students liked him and that was what mattered to him. As he saw it, his ability to do his job depended on maintaining good personal relations with the students. That was how he kept them coming to school and while there behaving moderately well. Even while he was suspending one girl, she was showing him the pictures of her newborn niece. The conversation, which included a reprimand, a suspension, and a discussion of the baby's virtue, was a little bizarre, but what mattered was that he liked her and she him. That liking prevailed over everything else. It was not rules, regulations, and policies that made these schools work; it was the myriad personal relations between staff and students, and the differential application of discipline procedures was a reflection of that fact. One can understand the conflicts that arose between adhering to the policies and procedures, as written, and working from the basis of good relations. It was not surprising that there were differing perceptions of the way discipline and attendance were or should have been implemented.

The personal element interjected itself into instruction in the same way. In the absence of a genuine interest in the acquisition of positive knowledge on the part of many students, the basis for getting along with students in class was not the subject matter per se, or even some future time when the student would possess the skills needed to hold a position in the work force. The basis was the good personal relations between teacher and student. "Get along with the kids" was not merely good advice designed to help smooth out the instructional and learning processes, it was the basis of the relationship between staff member and student. In fact, as I will argue in the next two chapters, it does not seem to matter *how* one gets along with students, only that one does.

There was a second matter that tended to confuse the administration of rules and regulations in all these schools. In fairness to the administrators, they were more limited in their approaches to discipline than teachers thought they were. It was one thing to demand a parent conference, but the truth was that many of the parents had no more (and frequently less) control over their children than did the teachers. Regarding the student who proclaimed she could "get around any old administrator" and who told the teacher what she thought of him, the class, and the school, a parent conference was called. As the teacher related it, "The father sat there, his hands folded between his legs and never looked up, and J. [the vice principal] said to the girl, "Did you say that" and she said, 'Yeah, I said it and I'll say it again, f— you, f— this class, and f— this whole place,' and the father didn't say one thing." At another conference, a student who had called a teacher an "old bitch," when reprimanded by his mother in the conference, responded by calling her an "old bitch." Parent conferences, while they may sound good, were not always effective with that set of students who needed them the most. Many parents of teenagers, even the well intended, have little control over their children.

> One girl came in with her father and I told her that if she skipped again I was going to suspend her and she just sat there looking down and he [the father]

looked at her and said, "You're just going to have to come to school." And she just sat there and he said; "Betty, look me in the eye when I'm talking to you so I get some understanding that you hear me." And she looked up, but she had an expression that told me she was going out that door as soon as she could. Now she's gone.

And too, it could not be assumed that the parent would side with the staff. Rudy was uncontrollable. He would perpetrate some act of violence, for example, throw a chair at someone's head, and claim he was acting in self-defense. In the conference, the parent agreed that her son had a perfect right to throw that chair at someone's head.

These conferences were often hard to arrange. In that industrial area, many students had both parents working in one or another large factory, and to get one of them to come into school for a conference was not that simple. The plants did not allow people to simply put down their tools and go to a school conference. So while some teachers did not believe that the administrators "set the right tone" or "backed them up," there was a feeling on the part of some administrators that some teachers did not have a sufficient appreciation of the difficulties of their role or the limits of their authority. A teacher might want a troublesome student moved to another class, but the administrators were leery of doing that because it might not be fair to the receiving teacher. And frequently some teacher would want a student thrown out of school, or would fail to understand why a student could not be thrown out of school. But the administrators are very aware that in general, education has been defined by the courts as a property right. One can be deprived of a property right but it has to be a matter of some seriousness and actions taken to deprive him of that right have to follow the rules of due process:

> A student's legitimate entitlement to a public education is a property interest which is protected by the due process clause (of the 14th Amendment) and which may not be taken away without adherence to the minimum procedures required thereunder.[5]

In all three schools, particularly Factory High and Suburban High, the administrators were very careful about expulsions, and if they did try to expel someone they were careful to attempt to comply with the rules of due process. The student had to be given notice of the charges, a hearing had to be set, and the student was allowed legal counsel as well as the right to present oral and written evidence. Hearing officers had to be appointed, transcripts kept, and appeal to higher courts was a possibility. The administrators really tried to avoid getting into such matters, which were of necessity time consuming, expensive, and potentially embarrassing to the school, which based its legitimacy on its ability to appeal to everyone. It was procedurally complicated to throw students out. At Factory High there was an incident the previous term when a boy had literally knocked out the principal by hitting him from behind with a heavy textbook while the principal was talking to some students in the halls. The police officers knew the boy who did it, the principal knew who did it, some of the students knew who did it, but the rules of evidence demanded witnesses who would attest and there were none. The students would not testify, the principal was hit from behind and did not see his assailant, and the boy was still walking around the school. This was indeed an unusual occurrance, but the lesson of the boy's continued presence was not lost on anyone. There were students who pushed drugs; people knew who they were. The students knew and would tell certain teachers, the police certainly knew, and the administrators knew; but it was not easy to catch them and prove it in a legalistic manner.

Not only were the administrators bound by rules of due process when dealing with the more serious cases, they were also limited by their own role in districts where the prevalent attitude was that the school should accommodate the child. In fact, it was clearly stated in the board policies of that district:

> If children fail to develop and grow as we reasonably expect they should, the shortcomings or errors should be focused on the structure of the system and community and not upon children. The school district must recognize and support the notion that the educational system is operated by adults with power, available resources, and control and therefore, children do not fail to learn, the schools and other community components fail to educate.[6]

With a philosophy like that accepted by key people in the district, the administrators had to give the benefit of the doubt to students, even when it was certain that they were guilty of assaults or drug dealings. An additional unstated safeguard was the activity of some quasipolitical black groups in the community who were quick to bring on the charges of racism when they thought that the "white administrators were picking on the black kids." If administrators did not throw troublesome students out, what could they do with them but put them back in classes of the sort from which they had been ejected? It made teachers unhappy, but they had little choice.

These school people had an interesting way of talking about their own role and the role of the school relative to the students. The phrasing was always in terms of "fulfilling the needs of the kids." The "needs of the kids" were never defined in any substantive terms. In fact, they seemed to be theoretically, at least, unlimited. If a child were misbehaving or chronically truant or unable to comprehend the material, there was the tendency to suggest that the system was not "serving that student's needs." That is not to deny that the school had procedures and requirements, but those procedures and requirements were always on the defensive against the accusation that the "needs of the kids" were not being served. The administrators themselves had internalized the "needs of kids" perspective and were sympathetic with even the worst students. They knew that some of them had terrible home lives and had no one who ever cared much about them. Many had been passed around from family to family. It was not, as some like to say, that they were from "single-parent homes." Many were from no-parent homes where the only adult was a slightly older brother or sister. It was the job of the school to try to help them by teaching them some skills and giving them some responsibility. Hence the emphasis on attendance, or at least trying to treat them civilly, something that many students may never have experienced outside school. Even with the toughest students the administrators maintained that their job was to "work with" and do everything possible to avoid throwing them out. As it was reasoned, if the school threw them out where would they go? The streets? The welfare rolls? Pregnancy and ADC? Eventually jail?

There were two additional elements. One was the matter of finance. The school districts received their state support money on the basis of the number of pupils in the school. That had not always been the case. In that state, twenty-five years previously the money had been allocated to schools on the basis of children living in the attendance area, not necessarily attending school. But that was changed, and now state money is allocated on the basis of pupils in attendance, not children living in the attendance area. So if a student were expelled the district would simply lose those funds. People in central administration were concerned about that. In fact, when the ninth-grade principal went for an expulsion, he was pointedly reminded by a central office administrator that he already "had forty-five for the year." "I never count 'em," he replied, but he did count them and he understood the pressure. The central office administrator may have been reflecting an additional element, the public relations of the district. As the superintendent of the suburban area explained, "you don't get people to vote their financial support by throwing their kids out." Up and down the system there were a number of pressures on administrators to retain and try to help all the students, even those that caused the most trouble.

Some of those students did cause a great deal of trouble. There are no other institutions in our society that I know of that will put up with some of the behaviors that urban public schools put up with. The police officer's desk in Factory High was an interesting place. In it were some air guns, a large number of knives, clubs, and brass knuckles that he had taken from students, and he didn't even show me the guns, which had been taken to the station house. According to him there were at least two students in that school who had murdered people, and one of them had committed two murders. The boy who hit the principal in the head with the heavy textbook was, in the year of the study, sent to prison for five counts of rape and one of abduction. On one particular Friday afternoon when I was in the police office, a call came saying that "Philip went home to get a machine gun to kill Luther in some argument over a girl." They became quite excited and started looking for Philip all over town, because they knew that his father dealt in contraband weapons and his threat to "get a machine gun to kill Luther" was not just idle talk. He had the access to and had used a machine gun before. One student, a reputed pusher, was the son of a big-time drug dealer and already had the car, the clothes, the ready money, and according to the police, had a series of girls who were also students working for him in that school. (According to the police officer, "That's all right, he's destined for a short life.") And around the back hung the dregs of the community because of the access to action and to girls. On occasion some of those young adults, most of them former students, came into the building and caused some damage or assaulted someone. On one occasion the tenth-grade principal spent three days looking for a nonstudent who had assaulted three people with a club and was still walking around among the 2,400 students.

It wasn't just a matter of controlling the students, it was a matter of keeping orderly a place where any number of incidents could develop from any number of places. One big fight was fomented by a family squabble in which the grandmother had tried to kill a neighbor. On numerous occasions, the gang wars of the community came into the school. Once three former students who had been expelled came to the school area as the buses were leaving. One block from the school they fired a pistol into a bus carrying some members of the rival gang. They missed their rivals but hit a ninth grader in the face. Another time a group of boys took a special education girl, forced her into a van, took her to a house, and according to the girl "did things to me," and then "tried to get me to do those things with other people for money."

Administrators who dealt with such matters felt that teachers did not appreciate the difficulties they faced and were sending them petty matters that they should have handled themselves. "Honest to God, she sends kids in here because they forget their pencils." One could clearly see the conflicts between the perceptions and obligations of teachers and the perceptions and obligations of administrators. One time in the police office in an idle conversation, a particular math teacher was telling how he had caught a boy cheating and had reprimanded him for it. "Do you know who you were talking to?" said the police officer. "That kid killed two people that we know about and we don't know how many he killed that we don't know about. We just can't prove it." After a few more minutes of listening to the officer explain the history of that particular student, the teacher remarked that he did not know anything about that world. "I have my classes, my computers, this is a whole different reality." It was, and both went on within the same building at the same time. Considering the difficulties inherent in such schools, one can see the potential for conflicts between teachers concerned about the acquisition of positive knowledge and administrators pressured by their own belief in the necessity of doing something for students, and further pressured by the central office, community, and funding processes to retain everyone. As one teacher explained:

> This girl missed 55 days of class, 55 days and she hadn't handed in an assign-
> ment since I checked my book, since October 10, and so I flunked her from
> the class. But the parent came in and talked to the principal, so I got called
> in and he said, looking right at me, "Mr.—is it necessary to fail that student?"
> and I said "yes" and showed him what I'm showing you, and then he looked
> at me and said again, "Is it really necessary to fail that student?" I said "yes"
> but the third time he said it, I got the message.

The message was simple. Getting along with and keeping the students in class and somewhat orderly is more important than seeing that they acquire some substantive positive knowledge. Like most, that particular teacher would like to have done his teaching from a subject-matter stance, would like to have students who cared enough about the material to come to class and hand in the assignments, or at least would have liked to have some sanctions to invoke against those who refused to do either. But he did not have that kind of authority. It was more important to keep them in school, in class, and in order than it was to teach them something and see that they learned it. He understood that. As he later put it: "What can you do when you have to take everybody and keep them all happy?"

Of course he was frustrated. Many teachers were, and the way they accommodated to the situation is the topic of Chapter 3. But in general it seemed to me that in all the schools, the sum of the constraints from outside the immediate school made the priority to attract, retain, and keep students orderly. The administrators went to considerable lengths to attain that end and they pressured the teachers to follow their example.

Some of this makes these urban schools sound disorderly, but they were not. The teachers were competent and knew how to manage students at the same time they instructed them, the administrators who accepted the referrals and ran the organization, the hall guards who watched the doors, and the police officers who were there for the more serious matters were all capable if not of preventing assaults and drug usage, of at least dealing with them competently. Their efforts were sufficient to keep those elements from disrupting the school. The buildings were clean, the halls and lavatories well lighted and relatively safe, and the school grounds relatively free of drifters and pushers. But that took a tremendous effort on the part of those people and a tremendous amount of organizational resources. If we just calculate the cost of salaries and benefits at Factory High for a principal and four assistants, two police officers and three hall guards and four administrative secretaries, the figure in 1979 was approximately $300,000, all to "keep the lid" on that one urban secondary school.

The same held true for Urban High, where all the extra resources went into maintaining order and attendance under conditions of animosity between blacks and whites. Consider the all-white suburban school of 1,600 students. There were two assistant principals who spent most of their time on attendance and discipline, seven hall guards, one truant officer who was also in charge of the hall guards, and two attendance secretaries. Also, there was a police liaison officer paid by both the police and the school district who spent most of his time on cases involving students. There too the administrators valued most the teachers who "got along with the kids" and did not burden an already busy office staff with additional problems that they should have handled themselves. There was also the pressure to keep the parents happy and the students in school. It happened that year in Surburan High that some boys damaged some teacher's cars, and when they were confronted by an assistant principal, responded by threatening that person's adolescent son. One would think that such behavior was unacceptable, but when it was talked out with the principal, they promised "not to do it again" and everything was dropped. Overall that was the way such things were handled. If such an incident were pressed it might result in poor publicity for the school and resentment on the part of the boys' parents, who were voting taxpayers. If they were expelled, the school could lose the state aid. Perhaps most important, expulsion of such students would violate the staff members' own perspective that the school should preserve the egalitarian ideal by serving the needs of all the students, even those who appear to need most some improving of their behavior. One does not serve those "needs" by throwing them out of school. If a relatively small number of them were thrown out of school, then there would be many fewer attendance and discipline problems and fewer resources allocated to maintaining order. But that is not the way these public schools operated. Their commitment was to "everyone" and they did what they could to serve "everyone," even to the point of directing a tremendous amount of the available organizational energy to just keeping order. One does not serve students by throwing them out of school.

Devouring a great deal of organizational time and energy was only the first effect of the problem of attendance and discipline. A second and more far-reaching effect (which will be addressed in the next chapter) was not only did the administrators spend their time and energy on those issues, but they pressured the teachers to "get along with kids" and not send them to the office, where they would be an additional burden on the already busy administrators. And they valued most those teachers who were best at it, least those who could not do it at all.

The most commonly heard negative comment about one or another teacher by an administrator was that he or she "didn't seem to like kids." That meant that the teacher was unable to maintain cordial relations with them in the classroom. Such a situation could not only burden the administrators, but in the biracial schools could lead to just that kind of racial incident that everyone feared.

In effect, according to the thesis, the instructional and curricular side of the two urban schools was subordinate to maintaining attendance and discipline. As the reasoning went, if students were orderly then at least they were in school and not on the streets. As many of the staff believed, if they could be kept orderly they would at least be learning "that," which was more than they would learn on the streets. Many administrators felt that if the students learned to show up on time and stay orderly, the school was doing its job. As Mr. D. (whom I quoted earlier) said, "The worst thing kids can do is . . . walk in, look around, and decide, 'Well, I don't want to be here, I think I'll go home.'" Teachers simply had to get along with students in class, and the way they did that is the subject of the following chapter.

SUMMARY

These descriptions of events are taken from two studies, one of which was designed to examine patterns of interaction between black and white students in an urban school. We found a great deal of latent and manifest animosity between blacks and whites, animosity which occasioned innumerable small acts of violence and always threatened to occasion a general outbreak of violence. The major effect of those incidents and that general threat was to force the administrators into spending almost all of their time and energy "keeping the lid" on these schools. Not only did administrators have to spend their time and energy in that direction; they evaluated other elements of the school (e.g., teacher performance, activities, scheduling) from that same perspective. What contributed to the maintenance of order was valued; what failed to contribute was not valued. One of the things that contributed was keeping students apart; therefore, what kept them apart was valued.

The second effect of biracialism was that it worked against the creation of any common norms or communal perspective or consensus among the participants. While race was only one of the elements that divided the students, it was the most visible and potentially dangerous of those elements and hence the one singled out for the most attention. The students, as much as possible, were kept apart, kept moving, and kept under constant supervision, all of which prevented them from coming together in a way that might have proven dangerous.

The main effect of biracialism was that it increased the potential for trouble; it was not treated directly, but rather as part of the general problem of discipline and attendance. Looking closely at those two biracial urban schools, as well as a suburban school, we well understood both the pervasiveness and importance of maintaining order and attendance among all the students. That basic fact of school life can be traced to the obligation of the school to provide some sort of instruction for everyone so that none may be denied equal access to social, economic, and political equality. That ideal is what legitimizes our public schools and undergirds the major structural constraint of taking everybody and maintaining order among them.

NOTES

1. J. Conant, *The American High School Today* (New York: McGraw-Hill, 1959), p. 17.
2. School board policy of Factory High School District, 1964.
3. "A Public Inquiry into the Status of Race Relations in the City of—," State Civil Rights Commission, 1968.
4. L. Cosar, *The Functions of Social Conflict* (New York: Free Press, 1956), p. 156.
5. 529 F. Supp. at 172 (N.D. Texas, 1981), in *West's Education Law Reporter*, 1982, 2(3): 417.
6. School board policies of Factory High School District.

3

The Curriculum, Part I

INTRODUCTION

Chapter 2 described briefly the communities and the schools, but concentrated on the pervasive issues of biracialism, attendance, and discipline. In the urban schools, more resources were allocated to those areas; in the less tough school, fewer. But no matter how many administrators there were in a school (two in the suburban, four or five in the urban), their primary responsibilities dealt with attendance and discipline. School people have taken very seriously the admonition from communities to keep their schools safe, orderly, and attended. Above all, that is where administrative efforts are directed. But such efforts are costly not only monetarily but also in additional ways. Attendance and discipline requiring what they do, there was very little supervisory or administrative time left for matters of instruction, evaluation, or curriculum. There was a corresponding pressure on teachers to "get along with the kids" and not add to the long list of petty issues that made their way to the administrators' offices. What administrators wanted were teachers who liked and related to the students, who had few discipline problems, or who at least handled those they had themselves. Beyond that it seemed that they asked little of the teachers, leaving them alone as individuals to work out their own patterns of instruction, patterns that went unscrutinized as long as there was no trouble or rumor of trouble in their classes.

The thesis is that the combination of these two factors, the taking up of administrative time with attendance and discipline and the corresponding pressure on teachers to handle their own classes in their own way so long as they did not create problems or further burden the administrators, created a situation wherein teachers were left alone to handle curriculum and instruction not as a faculty or department, but as individuals, each to himself, each allowed to create, implement, and evaluate his classes the way he saw fit. If that is true, then it says a great deal about curriculum, about these schools, and perhaps about the definition of an education. Since it is a rather different way of viewing curriculum and instruction from what we are accustomed to, this and the next chapter will be devoted to explaining it in the context of the schools studied. Some of the descriptions will be of less-than-successful classes, but this is not done to criticize the schools or the teachers. My purpose is to explain and discuss the structure of these schools as organizations, and it is by looking at the extremes of behavior that we can understand and outline the limits of that structure.

All the schools we studied were comprehensive, that is, founded on the premise of serving a large and diverse set of students with different educational experiences under the same roof. The curriculum was organized around what were assumed to be the "needs" of the students. This issue of student needs is quite complex and will be returned to a number of times throughout the book. Understandably vague, it stems from some equally vague assumptions; for example, that the school exists to fulfill the educational aspirations of all the students, that all young people need an education in order to survive and succeed, and that all should obtain that education in school. Beyond that there is the official assumption, useful in a democratic society but questioned by experienced teachers, that the acquisition of positive knowledge is or can be made interesting and appealing to everyone. Faced with the necessity of having to provide some sort of abstract positive instruction for everyone, and armed only with the limited assumption that everyone wants it, the staffs of those schools embarked on an endless search for something that would interest each of their students. If that something could be found, then it was reasoned that the student's "educational needs" were being met. While curious, this line of thinking does have a certain logic about it, and that logic formed the basis of the curriculum in these schools.

THE CURRICULUM OF THE SCHOOLS

The schools I studied had a large number of courses organized around departments; a few courses were required, most were electives. In Factory High, with five periods a day, five days a week, a student could complete forty credits of course work during his high school years (four years, two semesters a year, five periods a day), but only thirty-four credits of course work were required for graduation. The requirements were eight semesters of English, four of history, two each of science and mathematics, two of physical education, and one of government. So one had to take only nineteen credits of required work, which left twenty-one credits for electives.

This large number of courses was divided into levels of difficulty. Given the number of electives in any area, and the division into levels of difficulty, there were in Factory High with 2,400 students thirty-one separate courses available in English. In Suburban High there were twenty-seven. To satisfy the English requirement in Factory High, one might choose Shakespeare, mythology, tradition and revolt in literature, music as expression, speech, yearbook, newspaper, drama, mankind's voice today, investigative paper, mystery stories, man-to-man, philosophy, mass media, learning center (an option for illiterate or marginally literate students), what's happening (a second option for the same students), troubleshooter (yet a third), developmental English, black literature, grammar, careers, journalism, social problems, mastery learning project, writing, American literature, or simply English 32. In addition to thirty-one separate courses in English, the school also offered sixteen options in social studies, twelve in math, fifteen in business, ten in vocational training, eight in science, eight in art, seven in music, and three in home economics. Physical education, driver education, and co-op education were also available, as well as a very extensive set of offerings for students of "special" status.

In Suburban High there was an equally interesting array of courses. To satisfy a requirement for social studies in this school, one might take world history, economics , psychology, sociology, anthropology, state history, or history of World War II. These schools also offered students the chance to attend an area career center to study advanced courses in welding, hairdressing, laboratory work, woods, metals, building trades, secretarial work, and data processing. Other students could and a few did attend the local community college for advanced work in math or science or arts, and both of those schools had a few classes wherein students could earn advanced college credit.

Unlike Factory High, where the day was only five periods long and ended at 12:45 P.M., Suburban High had an eight-period day. There it was possible to graduate in three years, while it took at least three and one-half years to graduate from Factory High. Suburban High's more flexible day enabled third- and fourth-year students to leave the building as early as the end of the fifth hour (11:15 A.M.) to go to paying jobs, for which some of them were receiving high school credit through the co-op program. Two-thirds of the seniors and one-half of the juniors availed themselves of that option. In addition, in either school a student after his seventeenth birthday could take a full daytime job and attend evening school.

In both schools, one had to accumulate from seventeen to twenty-one credits, but the required courses were minimal. At Factory High students had to take ninth-grade civics, one year of general math, one of science, three of English, one of physical education, and one of social studies, but which of the optional courses that a student took within each of those areas was entirely up to him or her. The state requires only that the student take government. The North Central Association, which accredited both schools, says only that a basic program of language arts, science, math, and social studies, foreign language, fine arts, practical arts, and physical education be "offered." It says nothing about requirements or about all the options. Its position is very explicit: "It is the responsibility of the school[s] to plan their own curriculum patterns to serve their own students . . ."[1]

One might ask about the nature of the total curriculum, or the premises upon which these classes were created, or even by whom they were created. All of that will be dealt with presently. For now we will simply say that the curriculum of these schools was diverse and that diversity was justified in the name of serving the needs of diverse students, or the diverse needs of students—it is not clear which. The school exists to serve the "needs" of the students but the needs have never been defined in any substantive way. The process of diversifying the curriculum seemed to go on by itself while it remained for the student, individually, to decide which eight of the thirty-one English courses he or she might want to take. Of course the curriculum was not completely open. Each school had some guidance counselors to assist with the decisions, and they attempted to put students in appropriate classes. Suburban High had three-and-one-half counselors for 1,600 students, Factory High had two counselors for 2,400 students, Urban High had three counselors for 1,900 students. But in addition to advising students these counselors worked with the testing programs, did personal counseling, and kept the extensive student records. Advising was only one and not necessarily the most pressing of their tasks. They were also restricted in their role as advisors because of the prohibition against formal tracking. This was an interesting issue because it illustrated some conflicting forces to which the schools were subject.

While formal tracking was prohibited, only the better students took Mrs. P.'s ethics class, where they read and discussed literary classics, and only the poorer took "Girl Talk," where they learned to spell and practice writing simple sentences around the themes of their personal lives. Only the brighter took calculus or math functions and only the slower took foundations of math, where they struggled to learn to add and subtract, multiply and divide. "I mean, of course, they're tracked. Those counselors know what they're advising and they make sure the bright kids go in mythology—the slow ones in Girl Talk. But at least we've offered them the opportunity. We've put it on a piece of paper that they can take Mrs. P.'s ethics class. If they decide not to, that's their responsibility." And it was the student's responsibility. One could sign up or refuse to sign up for any given class; it was entirely up to the student. By creating such an open system wherein (except for math or foreign languages) students were free to elect what they wanted, the staff could demonstrate that they were not only trying to satisfy the needs of every student, but they were not preventing anyone from fulfilling himself. What could not be tolerated was the accusation that they were forcing the black students into the lower classes.

According to the counselors, it was not so much a matter of keeping students out of the harder classes as it was trying to get students into electing them. In fact, in all of the schools there were a number of counselors and teachers who expressed concern over the unwillingness of the students to elect the harder classes when they were free in a nontracked system to select the easier ones. As one explained, "Most kids just want to know what they have to do to get out of high school. They want to come to school all right, but they're not aggressive about it. . . . A few kids have parents who push them. I had this one girl and her parents told me to 'push college' so I wrote 'push college' right on her folder and tried to get her in the college prep classes, but she wouldn't do the work and would do anything to get out of the hard classes. . . ." There is little he could do about it.

With the options enlarged and the students left to choose their classes and tracking prohibited, the more academic courses (physics, chemistry, calculus, etc.) were not being subscribed. In Factory High the advanced vocational courses were not well subscribed. The teachers' explanation in all of the schools was in terms of the clientele, and particularly in those schools which had gone from predominantly white to predominantly black, the explanation was ready made. "The Jewish kids left, all at the same time, and they were the ones who took the courses." "These kids don't have anyone at home who cares about their education." "They don't have the motivation." "They can't read when we get them." "It's not their fault, they don't have a tradition of reading and writing." In the school where the students were predominantly white and working class, the explanations were only slightly different. "They're blue collar." "All they want to do is go to the factory." "Their parents don't care." "Cars are more important."

There was an accentuating element to this phenomenon of the harder classes being difficult to subscribe. It was estimated by the teachers in Factory High that of the 2,400 students only 200 were the type who would enroll for the harder classes, a number that according to them was growing smaller every year as parents of the able students took their children to the suburbs or to private schools. What that meant for the school was that if one wanted to initiate a more academic class, say Shakespeare or Biology II, one was forced into competing with other teachers for the time and interest of those 200 students who had only five periods a day like everyone else. But if the teacher wanted to initiate a less demanding elective, there was a potential market of 2,200 for whom to compete. Not only did courses proliferate, but the proliferation was of less demanding courses for less able students.

But at least tracking and the accompanying discrimination against black students, poor students, and particularly black poor students was avoided. Anything that remotely resembled that would have been unacceptable in those communities. There was still a residue of bitterness left over in the black communities from former times, when whites were tracked into the higher, blacks into the lower classes. It was not only a residue. Some blacks still suspected that it went on, and maintained that the recently initiated special education classes were designed primarily for their children. The people who wished to maintain such accusations could usually get some public forum from which to launch them, and the administrators in the urban schools were under constant pressure to prove that they were doing nothing of the sort. The open elective system with its proliferation of classes was part of their answer to the accusation.

In addition to ameliorating some external pressures, that system helped solve some internal constraints. No one in any position of authority in the school had to decide whether Algebra III was more important than welding or welding more important or useful than social studies. If decisions about the worth of courses had to be made, they would conflict with the teacher certification offices of the state or the teacher's contract agreement, neither of which discriminated among the worth of individual teachers or individual subjects. A teacher is a teacher, a subject is a subject, and subsequently, a high school education is a high school education. Perhaps the free market system outside the school will discriminate. Perhaps some colleges will discriminate, but no one speaking for the school does. Rather, the system is left open and elective, and these schools as entities abstained from any judgment which could put them into conflict with or alienate some segment of their paying population, or put them into a position of having to make pejorative judgments about some student's education.

In effect, the pieces fit. The need for community good will, the need to avoid any action that could be construed as making negative judgments about the black students' abilities, the leveling effect the union had on the set of teachers in each school, the need of the school to be responsive to a large number of groups who want to expand the curriculum in this or that direction in order to serve particular students—all combine into a system where a large number of students were offered a very large number of courses and told that they could take what they liked and call it their high school education. It is a curious system, but there is a definite logic to it and it satisfies the constraints operating on the school.

TEACHERS AND CLASSES

The matter of curriculum is essential because it is at the center of what we call a high school education. I will discuss it at length in Chapter 4 when I attempt to explain how teachers decide what they will or will not do in the classroom. For the remainder of this chapter, I want to move away from the organization of the school and the constraints that act on the organization and its administrators and begin to discuss the constraints on teachers in their classes.

For the teachers in all of the schools, the day was filled with students. Each teacher, by union contract, had to teach five classes on each of 180 school days per year. One had his five classes of math, physical education, science, music, or art, and so forth. In some schools there was also one additional period in which he or she was expected to do a duty assignment

in the corridor, study hall, or cafeteria; one lunch period; and one preparation period. Between periods, the schedule allows for five minutes passing time during which classes were to be ended, other classes prepared for,
audio-visual machines to be moved about, books to be put away or laid
out, a smoke, lavatory break, or any number of things to be attended to.
But most of the teachers' time was taken up with student matters. Over
three-quarters of the teachers' day by schedule and contract is spent in the
company of students, attending to their instruction, answering their questions, or just being in their presence. Students of course always outnumber
the teachers by some large number to one.

In addition to classes, duty assignment, or extra class, the teacher's
preparation period might also be spent in the company of students. In all
of the schools it was an ethic among the staff to treat students with patience
and courtesy. If two teachers were talking and a student approached one
of them, the student was always heeded. If a group of teachers were in the
departmental office adjacent to their teaching area and a student wanted
to see one, the student might or might not have been admitted, but he was
always attended to. If he was admitted, then whatever action was in progress stopped while he and the teacher were talking. If a group was gathered
in the vice principal's office and a student showed up with a request, the
interaction stopped while he or she was listened to. Wherever teachers
were in those schools, whether working, resting, or socializing, a student's
request was always heard. Courtesy to students was a common element
among the professional staffs of the schools, and while I observed very
different behaviors among the teachers, they all adhered to it. "We're here
for the kids." "You have to like the kids." "You have to get along with
the kids." "The kids are why we're here." "If you don't like the kids you
can't teach," were some of the ways they put it.

Because the hall periods were brief, the cafeteria period nonexistent in
two schools and brief in the third, the major setting for student-teacher
interaction was the classroom. The classes were structured so that the
teacher articulated the experience, doing most of the talking, questioning,
and moving about, while students sat, watched, waited, listened, and
spoke when spoken to. This pattern holds true for American high schools
in general, and our schools were no exception. The rooms were all square
and the chairs fixed in rows or occasionally semicircles so that all eyes could
be fixed on the teacher. The teachers, true to their subject matter specialty,
took that center position and used it to pass on the material that they
considered important. The expectation was that the teacher would have
the central role in creating the class, and everything was set up around that
expectation. The basic assumptions of subject matter specialty, downward
communication, and teacher centrality were never questioned.

But the subject matter of classes is more complicated. First, there is
the issue of the tenuous hold positive knowledge has on students. Just
because the teacher has some legal authority does not mean that the stu-

dents accept his or her leadership in matters of learning, and it certainly does not guarantee their interest in learning. In fact, for many students the subject matter of classes was of only marginal interest. Second, particularly in the urban schools, there was the matter of the very sensitive relations between black and white students. It did not take much to ignite the latent animosity that was always present. And once that animosity was out, the teacher could lose control of the class. This was particularly noticeable in a drama class at Urban High when the teacher wanted to discuss a movie he had shown the previous day.

There were four blacks in the drama class, Frank, his friend Raymond, one girl, and another boy, all sitting right next to the door. There were three white students down in the left-hand corner. There were five girls in the center; three more whites in front, one boy and two girls, and next to the stage where Mr. H. was standing, were three white girls. Mr. H. did not call attendance. He just started right off with, "What did you think of the play?" The play was something they had read about racism the day before. The original story had been about a Jew in a non-Jewish school who later entered the army with gentiles and found that he could not be friends with them. The play had been updated and the Jew had been changed to a black, who was thrust into an all-white situation.

When Mr. H. said, "What did you think of the play?" the four blacks had been talking together. Then they shifted down in their seats and did not say much. But the teacher was directing his questions at them, so Frank replied, "Unreal. It's just not a real situation. You just wouldn't find one black in the center of all those whites." Mr. H. tried again. "What did you think of the action of Morris?" (A white in the play who rejected the black). Again, the blacks shifted down and didn't say much. Some of the white students volunteered that they thought it was pretty good. Mr. H. had the attention of the three white girls in the center and talked to them a little bit about what they thought of Morris. Then he asked: "What did you think of John, the black?" Again, Frank volunteered, "I didn't think John was acting the way a black would act, because I didn't think you'd ever find one black in the middle of all of those whites, in that white place." Then Frank said, "Mr. H., I've got a question." "What is it?" "How come everybody hates whites? What is wrong with whites?" Mr. H. said, "Do you mean how come there is prejudice?" Frank said, "No, how come Chinese hate them, Africans hate whites, Indians hate whites, Spanish hate whites, how come everybody hates whites?" While Frank was talking it became quiet for the first time. Mr. H. tried to keep it on an academic level. He explained, "Sometimes we hate people when we don't know about them." At that the blacks all went, "Awwww, s—," and slumped down in their seats. But then Mr. H. asked: "Do you hate whites?" "Yes, I do." "What do you mean?" "I call myself a revolutionary." "You mean a militant?" Frank said, "No, not a militant, a revolutionary." At this the big white student down front broke in, "Do you mean you're prejudiced?" "No, I'm not prejudiced. I walk around here with a smiling face, I say hello to whites, I interact with them, I get along with them. But I'm a revolutionary, I wouldn't do anything for them. They come down to my neighborhood and they're on their own." The white student insisted, "You're prejudiced." Frank said, "No, I'm not prejudiced. I told you I'm not. I'm a revolutionary." The white student and Mr. H. asked him what he meant by that. As Frank explained it, he wanted to make the black race supreme in the United States. Their reaction was predictable: "Why should the black race be supreme?" "Well, whites were supreme. We were your niggers for a long time, we were your slaves, we had to hoe your gardens, haul your cotton. We're not going to do it anymore. We're going to be supreme." The whites at this time were getting excited, and the blacks were all with Frank. Some white girls insisted both races could get along. Frank's reaction was that he "had to come to your school, had to get along because it's your school. I go upstairs and see the 'man,' he's white. I go to your white hospital down the street and I see your white cops. But I'm just putting on a face. There's only one thing I'm for and that's blacks." One white girl said, "Well, they hate us because we're more advanced than they are." Frank didn't buy that. "Whites destroyed civilizations more advanced than theirs." Mr. H., who kept trying to keep the discussion on an academic level, explained it as exploitation because "richer whites exploited poorer blacks, which was a natural human way to behave." Frank didn't buy that either. He insisted there was something intrinsically wrong with whites.

Then Raymond broke in: "There's no such thing as being friends with a white man. There's no such thing as a black and a white being friends." One white girl spoke up. "We've got two blacks in our family." Raymond derided her: "What do they do, shine your shoes, do your laundry, carry the clothes?" "No, they're husbands. And they've got beautiful children." Frank laughed and slapped hands with Raymond. "They're not black, they're colored." Mr. H. asked the difference. He said, "A colored man will accommodate the whites, call them into his home, pretend to get along with them. A black will have absolutely nothing to do with them." Frank also said, "The thing about colored, they've got no pride. They've got no pride. The blacks have pride. I'm proud." Frank then repeated his former statement about putting on his face. The only thing he wanted he said, was "black power, black revolution, and black supremacy." All the blacks were together on this, clearly together. What was interesting was that all the whites, including the teacher, were banded together telling Frank he was wrong. It was just that obvious. As soon as some disagreement arose, the whites went with the whites, blacks with blacks. Then a girl down front said, "What about black guys and white girls?" Raymond got excited about that. "You know what they're after? They just want to take you out to see what you can give them. And that's all. You know George? All those white girls go after George. He didn't go after one of them, they were all after him. Yeah, and he done 'em wrong too, he done 'em wrong." The girl insisted that the black boys came after them, and she said, "They won't even keep their hands off of us." The blacks all hooted at that but the other white girls agreed. Then Frank got on the issue of who was calling whom a nigger, and who was calling whom a honkey. He tried to explain that whites and blacks are never really friends. He said, "We get along here, but when we go back to the blacks, we call you honkeys and you call us niggers." The whites denied that, but by this time the big white kid was standing over next to his friend on the left side, and they were whispering about something. Raymond said, "You don't have to whisper, say it out loud. Go on, say it out loud, say it out loud. Did you call me a nigger?" The kid said, "No, I didn't call you a nigger." Raymond said, "Yes you did, go on, say it out loud." The big white kid was red faced and frustrated. He said, "All right." Raymond said, "You called me a nigger—don't forget that. I won't forget that either." The other white kid said, "Is that what you're accusing him of, calling you a nigger?" Raymond said, "Yeah, you called me a nigger too." And the white kid said, "All right, consider yourself called . . ." (He didn't say "nigger," just "consider yourself called . . .") "Okay, I won't forget that, I won't forget that," Raymond said. "You ever come into my neighborhood I'll kill you . . ." From there it escalated, to talk of calling out older brothers and going home to retrieve weapons, but to the relief of Mr. H. and probably some others, the bell rang, and as angry as they were, the students took the opportunity to go their separate ways.

I went back to Mr. H.'s class the next day and I found him embarrassed about what had happened. That was understandable. At one point in the previous day's discussion he had tried to impose some order and had been told by a white boy to "shut up and let him [Frank] talk," which he did. On that following day the students broke into groups and worked on their parts. One group included two blacks and some whites, but Frank, Raymond, and Carol stayed by themselves. They too did their work, but only after a few brief and quiet remarks about having to "sit with them, them f—honkies . . . them white trash." But all—teacher, blacks, and whites— avoided the next step, violence. None seemed to be anxious to continue yesterday's disruption. Blacks went on interacting with blacks, whites with whites, the classroom was more boring than the previous day, but the students left their emotions out and there was no more talk of murdering one another. After seeing that I began to understand the futility of trying to discuss any racial issue rationally.

There is a related issue. One had to have more than just the material in order to interest and control the class. If the material failed to interest them and keep them in a state of order, or if it were taken amiss as it was in the drama class where the teacher lost the class, then one had to have something to fall back on. And what teachers had to fall back on was the good personal relations they had with the students.

An interest in acquiring positive knowledge was not sufficient to interest all the students, perhaps not even a majority, nor was it enough to bind these black and white students into working with one another amiably. One could not simply present material, even well-ordered and well-thought-out material, without considering the effect of the material on the class, the inherent animosity of blacks and whites, or the fact that some of the students cared little about learning anything abstract. Any one of those elements was sufficient to destroy the orderliness of the class. In the drama class it was the racial animosity that did it, but the other elements could have done it also. As indicated in Chapter 2, what a teacher had to do was maintain order and discipline and not further burden an already busy school office with his or her problems, take the chance of having it said that he or she "did not like kids." It sometimes happened that when the situations were potentially difficult, the overt subject matter of the class was relegated to a lesser importance, and the teacher relied on other elements to hold the class together.

In effect, the subject matter of a number of classes we witnessed was not so much art or drama or literature, but the personal relations between teacher and students. That makes sense. Even if the students did not care much about learning abstract knowledge, they were still quite decent and open to cordial relations with teachers. Since the teacher still had to keep twenty-five or so of them orderly for fifty or fifty-five minutes, then these cordial relations rather than the ostensible subject matter could serve as the basis for order. Given that, one could understand the sentiment behind the statements such as "you have to like the kids," "you have to get along with the kids," "we like the kids here."

What was particularly interesting in this regard was that in more than a few cases, there did not seem to be any subject matter other than the cordial relations. Mr. P. always came into fourth period about five minutes late, whereupon he would take attendance, exchange some banter with the students up front, then ask them how they felt, or respond to a personal question: "Hey, is your hair getting thin?" "No, man, it's just that I combed it different . . . Like it?" "Hey, whatsmatter? You look down." "Bucks lost, man, that's my team." "I didn't see the game—I had to do some work."

On this particular day the junior class president came in selling candles to raise money. George, with a big grin as always, mumbled a little to the class about the candles being on sale. The teacher felt he was ineffective and spent the next few minutes giving George a lesson in salesmanship.

"George, do these people know about your candles? You gotta tell 'em so they'll buy some. Come here."

George did not mind, and smiling broadly he gave the whole box to Mr. P., who took them out, laid them on the lectern, bought one himself, told the class about their quality, their construction, and the uses of candles, and sold three. "See, George, you gotta present your product so your customers will want them." Then he got on the subject of selling and told of an announcer on the radio in Chicago when he grew up who got so excited about presenting his product, Hamm's beer, that he drank a whole case of it during one ballgame.

By this time the period was twenty minutes old and while he was doing these things, the students were in what might generously be called a state of disarray. The sixteen students were partly listening, partly sleeping, and partly talking among themselves. It was not just on December 14 that Mr. P. avoided teaching. He followed a similar pattern every day we were in his class. Even if he did have some academic work that he considered important enough to mention, he would immediately leave it if something else came up.

One day he started on railroad mileage. Another teacher walked in: "Hey, I fixed your TV." "Oh, excuse me," said Mr. P., and walked out. Twenty minutes later he returned and he told us that he wanted to talk about the increase in railroad mileage between 1830 and 1940, and while he was reading the graph from the book not one student was paying a bit of attention. The boys up front were talking among themselves about basketball. William plays varsity. Raymond and Robert were in the center of the room listening to his assessment of the opposition. George had left after his usual short stay. The girls on the other side were either looking out the window or sleeping. One was angered by an earlier exchange with Mr. P., who asked: "You been taking those pills again?" "I ain't taking no pills," she replied.

John, one of the white boys in back, was reading a magazine, and of the two black girls in the back one was reading a novel, the other, looking bored, turned and asked me who I was. When I told her she said, "Don't you get tired of sittin' in these classes?" "Do you?" "Yes, we never do anything in here," and she showed me some novels she was reading. Another boy on my right said, "I wish they'd burn all these books, then we could have school on tape."

All the time the teacher was talking about railroad mileage. Some had their books open but did not look at them. Others just sat and stared or talked to their friends. This apparently didn't bother Mr. P. No individual was getting singularly disruptive so he just went on until even he became bored and concluded quickly that although "America has a lot of problems it is still the best country in the world."

While students openly admitted that they did nothing in there, some liked it. John told me: "Hey, you're trying to see all kinds of different situations, aren't you? Well, there's Mr. T., you should go to his class, it's the opposite of this one. He's real strict. Like, he doesn't take anything from the kids. Like, there's a line at the door and when the bell rings you're on one side or the other and if you're on the other he sends you out." "Do you like him?" "No, I hated him . . . I learn more this way— last year the kids just rebelled against him."

Mr. P.'s classroom behavior was somewhat unusual but not that extreme. There were a number of teachers who seemed to have little interest in the subject matter or the curriculum, and faced with a less-than-eager set of students had to find some way of relating to them for the fifty-five minutes. They would engage in a sort of random small talk which many students did not seem to find very interesting, as evidenced by the way they put their heads down or found a way to leave the class. But the students usually responded to such teachers with the expression: "He's a good guy." Many did not seem to be concerned about whether they learned anything or not.

A particular biology class was another good example of this. The teacher, after taking attendance for fifteen minutes, wrote a few phrases on the board: "Adam and Eve," "spontaneous generation," and "evolution," and told the students that: "For the next forty minutes you are to write an essay on how you think the world started, and here are three possibilities which you know, we discussed last week. I did this with my college prep class and they like it . . . It will do you good. Teach you to think for a change, which is something you don't do often."

I asked a student in the back, "Is this a college prep class?" "Noooo."

Then the teacher, having given his few directions, walked around, looked here and there at the students, who seemed to only half understand the assignment in the first place and were not doing much to finish an essay. Instead they sat and talked to their friends, or some fooled around. Two boys in the back were throwing things to the front. The teacher was not doing much to structure the situation. He had simply retreated from the center, leaving the students to their own devices. He also did what many retreating teachers did as time-killing devices. He walked around the room and engaged this or that individual or group in random bits of small talk, about a piece of apparel, a sporting event, a mutual acquaintance, or something they shared from some previous time. It was an interesting way of "nonteaching."

At the same time that these teachers were nonteaching, they sometimes tried to feed in didactic comments to whatever discussion or activity the students were pursuing, thus making some attempt to fulfill their role as teachers. Although they had retreated from a stance that involved clear expectations for students or themselves, they still hoped to teach the students something about something during that period. Or perhaps teach isn't the word; perhaps all they hoped to do was "relate" to the students.

Even those who did as little as I have described could make the case that they were teaching their students about the virtue of promptness, social relations, and self-control. They certainly were not hindering the students from obtaining their high school diplomas, because almost all of them would pass their students in those courses at the end of the term. So even with noninstruction many of the important goals of the school were being fulfilled. And of course these teachers were fulfilling what the administrators considered to be their major responsibility, that of getting along with students. They did not get upset if a student came late without the required pass, they did not fail students or send them to the office or foment teacher-parent conferences, or angry phone calls from students' parents. They did not add to the long line of students waiting in the office for attention, and that could be taken by administrators that those teachers "got along with the kids" or "liked kids."

This is not to say that there was not excellent instruction going on in those schools. There were many good and some excellent classes, a few of which I shall describe. But the argument will not change. The basic requirement for teachers was not that they instruct from some agreed-upon course of study. It was not even that they instruct. It was that they be capable of maintaining some state of moderate order among the students, and the proof that they could do that was that their students were neither running about the halls nor showing up in the office. One could instruct, one could not instruct; it was up to the individual teacher to decide how to conduct himself or herself in the class. The requirement in all the schools was that he or she be able to maintain order among the students.

The fact is, "not teaching" was one way to deal with a class, not a good way according to any learning theory, but a way that kept students orderly. No one disobeyed a direction that was never given, no one failed to hand in an assignment that was never assigned, no one flunked a test when there were none, and no student-teacher conflicts, fights, or cases of insubordination showed up in the office.

Also, if one were not teaching or if one were teaching less enthusiastically than he could, he would be less likely to anger students who could reciprocate by embarrassing the teacher. This is a hard subject to follow because staff members were reluctant to talk about it. But it was not uncommon for teachers to be intimidated and embarrassed by students whom they tried to motivate or to force into greater involvement with the subject matter.

"I was lecturing them one day and most of them hadn't done their homework and I don't know what I said to this one kid . . . a big black kid, you wouldn't want to meet him in an alley . . . but he stood up and he said, "What did you say, man?" . . . and I knew. Right then I quit assigning homework and lecturing. Now I put the assignments on the board and keep them writing at their desks. It's the only way." That teacher knew that one cannot just keep running to the office all the time to have his problems solved. Mr. L. knew it, too. In an algebra class, three boys and a girl were continually fooling around, talking, touching, and laughing. Mike seemed to be in the center. Mr. L. asked Mike if he could talk to him in the hall. They went out. A minute later Mike came in. "*Hurrrrmmmmph,*" he said, and slammed his books down on the desk and slammed himself into the seat and glared at the entering teacher, who, red faced and embarrassed, went on with the lesson while the four went on with their behavior.

Teachers who took an aggressive stance toward the material took a chance of incurring the animosity of the students, who, in that elective system, could be free not to elect one's classes. That had happened to a particularly demanding English teacher in Factory High. She was difficult ("old, crabby, bitchy, and hard nosed but a damn good teacher," as she herself put it), but a stream of students into the office complaining about her demands gave her a reputation among the administrators of "not understanding the needs of 'these' students." When her classes were no longer being subscribed, she was switched to home economics, in which she had a college minor but had never taught. Shortly thereafter she resigned from the system. A math teacher suggested to a girl who had not been coming to class or doing her assignments that if she insisted on taking a test she would probably fail it. The girl complained to her mother about the teacher's attitude, the mother brought it to the administrator, and the result was a reprimand for the teacher.

Student animosity could be turned into physical intimidation, as it did on a few occasions, or a student could embarrass a teacher, either in the class as Mike did or in the office by lodging a complaint with the administrator. But if the teacher's approach was tempered within the framework of good personal relations, that was less likely to happen. The obligation on teachers was to keep assuring both students and administrators that they "liked kids" at the same time they were instructing.

One thing was certainly clear. The teachers who did not teach were not being chastised by the administrators. I asked an associate principal in Urban High about the teachers being free to develop their own style: "That's the trouble, they're too free, they're free not to teach. They get in there and they talk about this and that and forget what it was they were hired for."

"But what do you look for in a teacher?"

"For a teacher who can handle himself personally in front of the class; a teacher who, although he might have a personal problem, wouldn't let it show. When he gets up in front of kids, I want him to make them believe that he really cares about his subject matter, whether he does or not. If he doesn't, that's all right with me. If he had some trouble that day, if he had some trouble with his wife, or he had some trouble with his family, I don't want it to show. I want a teacher who cares."

"But is discipline a common reason for not retaining a teacher?"

"In more cases than I would like to admit, that is true."

The principal was more specific. He wanted a teacher who maintained order, and a teacher who could not was "not welcome in the school."

I found a small number of teachers in all the schools who either never tried to teach or who tried it and then simply gave up but who were sufficiently astute to maintain their positions nonetheless. After all, as discussed in the last chapter, the administrators, busy with matters of attendance, discipline, and public relations, seldom came in to evaluate or supervise any of the classes (save of these nontenured teachers), and if there was nothing going on in a particular room they had no way of knowing it. Other teachers or students might have ways of knowing it, but there was no way anyone could do anything about it. An important structural element in all of the schools was that nowhere was there any provision for teachers exercising any scrutiny over their colleagues. Neither for students or teachers were the schools in any sense normative or communal societies. There was no case I could find of teachers exercising any pressure on a colleague to alter his or her classroom behavior.

So not only were the students allowed to work out whatever they wanted for their education, the teachers were free to develop their own approach to classes, with the primary responsibility that they maintain a reasonable state of order.

To strengthen the point, one could consider a class in Urban High wherein order was not maintained. The class was called "man in sports," an English elective for the "noncollege bound," as it was put.

There were twenty boys in the class, thirteen white and seven black, I sat down as I always did in the back. I asked a big, open-faced white boy if I was in someone's seat. "No . . . yeah, it's somebody's seat, but you can sit anywhere you want, nobody cares."

"What do you do in here?" "Nothing . . . we don't do anything in here. We never do."

He then pulled out a deck of cards, whereupon two black students came back and sat down, and he started dealing rummy. A few preliminaries . . . "Do you want to play?" It must have been the routine. There were two other card games going on in there. Most of the time the small group, social interaction is uniracial—black-black, white-white, never white-black—but here was an exception, one of the few I had seen. Others in the room were throwing things, literally: a book, a ball of paper. Others were walking around talking. One came back and confided in me, "This is the worst class in the school, but you'll get a good impression of what we do in here 'cuz these assholes wouldn't act different if the President was sitting back here." Mrs. H. came in, fussed with her books and papers for ten minutes while the students moved around, talked, played cards, and some just sat and did nothing—one read *Drag Strip* magazine.

"All right, everybody, sit down—today we have two oral presentations . . . First we have Fred." There was a lot of cheering at that, and Fred, a long-haired, lanky boy, got up and read his sixty-eight-word speech, which was about a pilot who was shot down in Germany territory and wised up to the fact that the Germans were pretending to be French. He read it with his head down, mumbling most of the time. The others were talking, playing cards, looking out the window; three were setting up a tape recorder. Mrs. H. tried to evoke a little discussion about the speech by asking Fred and others about the character, the plot, the element of surprise, but she got nowhere. Neither Fred nor anyone else cared or was willing to pretend he cared.

Then the open-faced boy got up and was supposed to run his tape, but he had forgotten it and had to go to the library to get it. "We can take a pause," said the teacher. Whereupon the action didn't change at all. Five minutes later he came back and he, the teacher, and the three others worked on the tape recorder for five more minutes before getting it going.

The tape took one and one-half minutes, and then Brian got up. "These are three poems that we liked from a book by John Keats." The recording was still going and ran into another section of the tape on which someone said, "And he ate a whole box of chocolate Ex-Lax," at which the whole class was briefly united in laughter.

To evaluate these presentations the teacher passed out forms on which the students were to write their opinions. I read a number of them as they were passed over: "It was good," "A+," "very interesting," "wonderful."

That was the end of class. For the remainder of the period we sat and continued the action that had been going on: card playing, talking, moving around, playing with the tape recorder. Two card games, one all black, one mixed, two boys throwing a ball across the room, a few talking, some sitting and staring.

The teacher walked around just as did other teachers; she would talk to a group of card players and asked them to prepare a presentation on card playing, turn to another group and tried to talk to them about next week's work, and picked up some papers that were deliberately thrown down by a boy, who then looked at her and told her he had not done it. She was trying to get some entrée into making the class a didactic experience, but it failed.

At the end of the class she confronted one student who was wadding up sheets of notebook paper and shooting baskets at the wastebasket. "How old do you have to be before you realize you're not to throw paperwads?" She was standing directly in front of him, her hands on her hips. He said, "I gotta catch the bus." She said, "Answer me. Don't you know the difference between right and wrong?" The student said, "Hey, get out of my way. I told you I had to catch a bus." "No, not until you answer me." At that the student gave her a light push and backing up she fell back over a chair. The student moved quickly out of the class and down the hall.

She picked herself up, walked over to me, and tearful and trembling said, "What can I do? I'm just new to high school teaching and I thought the latest thing was to have student-centered classrooms, so that's what I'm trying to do. What am I doing wrong? I work my tail off to try to be a good teacher; see these materials? I've collected all of them. I've been off a couple of years; but I'm trying to do what's best. I even took a business day to go across town and visit a teacher's class that everyone respects as a good teacher. I don't see anyone else doing that. Mr. M. came in one day to observe me, I'm trying to be student-oriented, see, that's the new approach, isn't it? And he tells me that the kids are too noisy and too many kids are walking around the room. So Mr. P. chews me out on Mr. M.'s recommendation. They tell me I'm not going to get tenure unless my classroom straightens up." (Her voice cracking, and her eyes watering.) "I'll tell you this—they gave me a poor evaluation and I'm bitter; all they're concerned about is quiet classes."

She was right, of course. The administrators could ill afford to put up with a teacher who had so little control over her classes and her students. In fairness they, too, cared about instruction and learning, but the constraints of their positions did not allow them to spend any significant time in those areas. On the other hand, she seemed to be just plain wrong in her assumption that her materials and student centeredness were sufficient to interest twenty or so adolescent boys, most of whom were in that class because they had a history of doing poorly in their previous years.

This was an extreme case, the worst I ever saw, but it is interesting that she did make more of an attempt to teach than some others. Although her organization and control were terrible, she did not retreat. The administrators did what they could for her, but since she was obligated to control the room by herself and unable to do it, she was judged unsuitable and released at the end of the term. That was not surprising, but others who did as little but were able to maintain some semblance of order through their good personal relations with the students and who did not burden the office with disciplinary cases were judged as being able to "get along with the kids" and were kept on.

So far I've argued that the principal obligation of the teachers in the schools I studied was to "get along with the kids." Operationally, that meant that they keep the students in a state of moderate order, maintain some cordial relations with them, and not send for administrative assistance. If they could do those things, then what they did beyond that in the way of instructing was up to them as individuals. But if a teacher chose to do nothing beyond that, he could still maintain his position on the payroll. An explanation of this may lie within the limits of the assumption about positive knowledge being interesting and appealing to everyone. The last teacher described believed it. She believed in her "open" classroom and had provided the boys with extensive materials, and had they been naturally interested in written communication or expression, they might have spent less time fooling around and might have come to pursue something sooner or later. Or perhaps the problem is not with the assumption but the assumption exercised in a traditional classroom setting. Whatever the limits, the material and the student's interest were not sufficient to make a class out of that aggregate. It took some personal rapport between the students and the teachers. That is the necessary condition for creation of a class.

A further illustration can be seen from a description of the students' behavior in the presence of substitutes with whom they had no relation. Faced with a long fifty minutes in a reputedly "difficult" class, substitutes often tried to throw out whatever if any plans the teachers had left, and organize a discussion around what they assumed to be the students' concerns. One young man, seeing that all the students were black, started right off telling them to read a story by Langston Hughes. "Ahh, we read that, we read that! We did that." "Let's have our group discussion. We didn't have it on Friday." The substitute asked, "What's a group discussion?" "Well, that's when we sit around and talk about things." There were only a few students who said this. Some of the other students were engaged in their own interactions; one girl was reading *Till Death Do Us Part*, by John Gunther; two other girls were talking; four boys were milling around; and some students were still entering. But the teacher agreed to the "discussion," so the students put their chairs in a circle and their books aside. The first thing the substitute said was, "What do you want to do?" What they wanted him to do was just be quiet, but he didn't. He felt he had to be the teacher, but they would have none of that. As soon as they got in a circle, Derrick started in on race relations and what was wrong with the world. The substitute would try to take Derrick's comments and structure them, but that isn't the way it worked. Derrick wanted to talk— not listen. The sub did not understand.

So Derrick would start talking and others would start talking right back at him at the same time, neither seeming to listen. That was the way the students conducted their discussions. If one watches it long enough one begins to understand that it makes sense and has a predictable order, but the sub was confused. He kept trying to get them to talk in firm, well-modulated tones, one at a time—like he was probably taught to do. He tried everything. He tried to tell them about his efforts in improving race relations through some organization and they listened for about a minute, but that did not interest them at all.

Then Berlin, the boy of whom Mr. D. had said, "He's a good kid but we missed the boat on him," came in. He handed the sub a slip and said, "I got thrown out of school." In an effort to be friendly the sub said, "I don't care." Berlin, in a very condescending slow voice said, "Look, I got thrown out last Friday and now I'm back and you have to sign this," as one would talk to a child. The sub signed the pass, turned, and tried to continue telling them about his Friday night; but their interest was gone, and Derrick began to berate Gerald (who was in Phi Psi) asking, "What does Phi Psi mean?" "Shhh, shhh, shh." Finally Gerald got everyone's attention so that he could tell them that Phi Psi was to get black kids together and do something for black people. Then Derrick yelled, "Well, if it is a black organization, how come you got a Greek name?" To which the boy replied, "Well, you're black, how come you got the name Derrick, that's a French name." "My name doesn't have anything to do with what's inside me." "Well, all our fraternities have Greek names, that doesn't mean that they have anything to do with what's inside us."

As soon as someone would say something everyone would go "Ohhhhhh," "Yeahhhhhhh," hoot and holler and yell at one another. Whenever the yelling would become loud and confused Raymond would jump up, get in the center of the room, do a little hi-life dance, collect the thrown pennies, and then sit down. Then they started "panning" one another's mother. One boy asked the sub, "Do you know what his mother did?" The sub was completely bewildered. "No." "His mother steals carburetors out of buses." Or, "You know that truck that turned over? Well, his mother turned it over." Then everyone would laugh. At one point the sub was reduced to standing in the center screaming at no one in particular: "*Quiiiieeeetttt . . . Quiiiieeeetttt . . . Quiiiieeeetttt!*" Mike looked at him and said: "Don't you yell at us." "Oh, I'm sorry. But I don't know how to get you to be quiet." "It doesn't matter, this is what we do on discussion days. Just don't yell at us."

In another class a substitute had no better luck. He tried the same tactic, but they didn't even stay in the room for him. He tried to keep them until the bell rang, and they wanted to go to the pep assembly. Everyone started crowding around the desk asking to be excused. The substitute said, "No, you have to wait, I'm going to take roll." They waited a few seconds and then said to me, "Ask him, ask him," They wanted me to tell the substitute that they could go. I said nothing but it did not matter. The students did not wait for my answer; they just went back to harrassing the sub. He was confused; he understood that he was being put on but he didn't know how or whom to accuse. Some of the students had legitimate excuses: one played in the band, another played ball, another was in the pep club, but all were saying at the same time, "I'm in the pep club man, I gotta go, we gotta be there." "I'm a cheerleader." "Sign this, sign it." But he wouldn't. So they started to go out without passes and he told them, "I'll call roll and give the names to Mr. T." They said, "You do that, you just do that," and four then walked out of the room, then two more, then one more, and then there were only six left. He called roll, but those remaining made excuses for the absentees so his threat was wasted.

A third substitute had an equally difficult time. The students started coming into the class and after giving her a quick glance, ignored her. Then they started to play cards. There were six of them right in front, others were talking and running around, coming in and going out of the room. She attempted to stop the card games and get them to watch a movie on prejudice. She haggled with them. "Come on now, we have to start, put the cards away, stop your card playing." They paid absolutely no attention, but she persisted and finally they went back to their seats and sat down. Then came the movie. It was about prejudice against Jews, Japanese, Catholics, and so forth. Of course, the black students saw no point in that—to them there was only one kind of prejudice. When the movie was over, she wanted to engage them in a discussion of prejudice, but it went nowhere. The students went back to talking among themselves, running around the room, playing cards, arm wrestling, and doing what they wanted. Referring to her plea to discuss prejudice, Mike said, "Lady, I've know that all my life; I've known it since I was fourteen and now I'm twenty-three." (Mike changed his age every week.) "You're prejudicing me against you right now," the teacher said. "Lady, there's the door; you can leave any time you want to." She then threatened to report the troublemakers to Mr. B. "Yeah, lady, you do that—go ahead." They knew he would ignore her report. After all, they liked him and he liked them and they had no personal relation with the substitute. She was of no consequence to either Mr. B. or the students.

Even when substitutes tried to implement the planned lessons, they were generally unsuccessful. It may have been a failure of the way they went about it. But more likely it was the fact that the students simply did not care much about the material and knowing that the substitutes had neither real authority nor personal relationships with any students, they had no incentive to comply with their requests. Students simply went about pursuing their own individual or group activities. On those occasions when the substitute would attempt to interest the students in something they were assumed to care about, he got nowhere. They were not to be seduced into a state of order by topics of assumed interest.

To those students the acquisition of positive knowledge was not in itself of sufficient interest to take up forty-five or fifty minutes. If it had been they would have at least paid some minimal amount of attention to the substitutes who tried to implement the lessons. The black students certainly cared about the racial questions but they refused to fit their concerns into the substitute's idea of classroom procedure. The same was true of white students. Faced with a long fifty minutes with the students, substitutes tried a number of topics, many of them of general interest to adolescents, but I never saw it work. The students have interests and passions to be sure, but those cannot easily be turned into topics for classroom discussion, or presented as problems with rational solutions which can be ironed out between 10:45 and 11:35. Each of these substitutes behaved decently and civilly toward students, probably knew the material, had at least some official authority, and most entered with the intent of teaching the subject matter. But the ones I saw always failed. Sometimes they could not even keep the students in the room. One could understand what teachers mean when they speak of "liking the kids" and "getting along with the kids." If one could not do that, he or she would have a hard time staying in the school.

This may be more true in those urban schools I studied than in other schools, where a greater number of students might have added reasons for being interested in the subject matter or might be a little more respectful of official authority. The classroom setting in those schools can be a difficult place for pursuing abstract topics in a cooperative manner. Ideally, orderliness in any setting emerges from some commonality of interest among the participants, who hold some view of themselves as engaged in a common endeavor. But in so many classes there was little of that. The size of the schools, the broad range of social and economic backgrounds of the students, the racial divisions all worked against the needed cooperation. The elective system was such that within single classes one would find sophomores, juniors, and seniors next to each other, which added to the general disparateness. People sometimes talked about cooperation; administrators sometimes spoke in public about the school as a community; but there was little to encourage it in the schools' structure.

The advantage of a cooperative, normative structure is that it can be called on by one, a teacher, trying to get another, a student, to do something she wants him to do. If they are both tied into the same general set of understandings about behavior, hers and his, then there will be fewer occasions for disagreement. But that was not the case in any of the three schools. The assumption was that education is an individually acquired entity. Not only was each student free to contract his set of classes, he was free to contract for his level of compliance in each class. (I want to distinguish compliance from achievement because the latter was probably dependent on abilities which differ naturally.) A student owed nothing to the school as an entity or the class as an entity. The result was that the teacher faced a class armed only with each students' presumed interest in the abstracted material. After all, it was an elective system and the students had elected the classes. Therefore, they should be interested. But that was a weak assumption, as some of the descriptions indicate.

An additional problem in many classes was the academic level of the students. Many of the students in those schools seemed to care very little for learning. Perhaps they cared more than was apparent, but many of them, particularly in the urban schools, had very limited skills. In Factory High only 37 percent of the tenth graders had scored an acceptable level on a statewide assessment test in math and only 47 percent had scored an acceptable level on a similar test in language. Therefore, all of the teachers had to teach classes with poor students. Some of the teachers were positive about the students, some less so, but all agreed on the students' general unwillingness or inability to do work outside of class. "You have to spoon-feed them." "They don't do homework." "They can't work by themselves." (Indicating an exercise which required fifty-four one-word answers.) "That's two days' class work for them. And if I ask them to do homework they don't do it. I gave them in-class homework and six of seventeen handed it in. I gave them out-of-class homework and two of seventeen handed it in . . . I don't know what they want; to graduate, I guess. I don't think they have any idea about learning." "I assign homework but it never comes in. I stopped assigning it." In effect, the lower-achieving students in that school seemed unable or unwilling to form an independent interest in the abstracted material. The cordial relations were not only the basis of maintaining order; they were equally essential to bringing the students along with the material because so many seemed unable to operate outside that relationship.

This "dragging them along" could be painful for teachers. As the biology teacher explained: "I can handle two or three nonreaders, but of the sixteen kids in here" (there were twenty-six assigned to the class but only sixteen came regularly) "ten of them can't read. You have to be so careful with them. You have to have everything set up as soon as they come in the door. If you don't they won't do it themselves. You have to be always helping them." At that time he was trying to help one girl. "A nonreader," as he said. She whined, claimed that she didn't understand, looked around, said she couldn't see anything through the microscope. He was positive and encouraging. He was known to like students and they him. But he was just dragging her along somewhere she did not want to go.

The advice given to teachers of lower-achieving students is that they individualize, and I saw it operate effectively in remedial math classes, remedial reading classes, and sometimes in independent study classes. The teachers seemed to be sufficiently well organized and the students sufficiently motivated to handle material geared to their level. But in other classes which demanded some complex tasks or some cooperative efforts or independent organization, it did not seem to work well. In one biology class, of the eighteen students, three were supposed to be working on their project but never stopped talking about their personal business. One girl wandered to the back, to a friend, to the teacher, finally picked up a gall ball and asked the teacher what it was. "It's a goldenrod gall ball that bugs use to protect themselves from the winter." "*Bugs*" . . . *Eeeeek*" and she ran laughing to the back of the room. Of the students there, only six did any sustained work during the period, and three of them were working on other classes. The students obviously liked him and he they. A number wanted to talk to him about rockets; one boy referred to him as "my favorite teacher," another said "he was the best teacher he had," and that mutual liking served as a way for him to keep some instruction in the dialogue. But it would be difficult to determine much independent interest in biology outside that liking.

An additional consideration about the classes with the lower-achieving students was that so many seemed slow and almost painful. Not only did the teacher have to pull everyone along within the framework of decent personal relations, but he had to overlook a lot that is not disorderly or disrespectful, but is distracting—the coming in late, looking around, walking to the front to get a paper or to the back to sharpen a pencil, the surreptitious eating, and putting down of heads. Not only does the teacher have to maintain the framework of decent personal relations, he or she has to pull the deviating students into some cohesiveness and at the same time keep articulating the experience.

It is not fair to leave these descriptions without describing at least one of the many excellent classes I witnessed. A number of teachers were quite successful in imparting a sense of importance of the subject matter, creating a sense of community and self-help among the students, and maintaing a strong posture toward the importance of acquiring positive abstract knowledge. In Mrs. S.'s English class, grammar was being taught to a group of juniors and seniors. There were seventeen students in the class, which was one of the neatest-running classes I have ever seen. In back of the room on the blackboard were listed the vocabulary for January 5th, 4th period, vocabulary for January 6th, 3rd and 4th periods. And on the bulletin board were a number of newspaper clippings, one about a boy getting his Ph.D. at the age of eighteen, another about getting jobs when one gets out of high school, another about college enrollment increasing; and there was a quotation from the Roman philosopher Seneca in the front.

On the table at the front of the room was a lectern and a desk piled with books. Mrs. S.'s housekeeper's sense of orderliness was obvious—in a school where almost all the desks were carved up, she was one who believed in preventing the defacing of furniture. She was fussing about it when I came in: "I just washed that desk." "That girl always writes on that desk." "I'll talk to her tomorrow." There were a number of blacks among the students in the room. Five of them were in the front center, three more by the back door, two by the windows. I always noted that because in most classes, all the black students clustered together in one or another part of the room, but here they were interspersed throughout the class.

Mrs. S. asked the one boy by the door, "Did you take your test yesterday?" He said no, so she gave him the test and told him to go down to the guidance office and take it. He left. Mrs. S. makes her own lessons. She handed out one sheet with a number of vocabulary words printed across the top (*maim, malice, mandate* . . .) followed by twenty sentences she had devised, the idea being that the student was supposed to put the correct word in each sentence. Ten minutes were devoted to privately working on this, during which time no one said a word. Then she gave back the previous day's tests and the students corrected one another's under her direction. She picked them up at the end of Wednesday's class and handed them out at the beginning of Thursday's class; the students corrected them and told her what the marks were or else handed them in after correcting them, and she got the marks from the test.

All the time she was doing this she assigned each student to read a sentence, or she'd call on somebody and say, "The English Winston Churchill's American ____," and they would fill in the word *namesake*. Her enthusiasm for the task was obvious. She seemed to genuinely like being there. She kept hovering over the entire class, coaxing, searching out the correct answers with looks and breath holding and gentle hints, chiding those who gave wrong answers.

With these techniques and her extensive preparation she kept complete control of everything that went on. The students, all of whom seemed to enjoy the lessons, were as completely "with" her as I ever saw them with any teacher.

Following the vocabulary lesson they took another test, which they then corrected. This test was on dependent clauses. On this one each person would read a sentence such as "The captain knew that the steps had been severely damaged in the hall," and the idea was to select the dependent clause, tell why it was a dependent clause, and what it depended upon. She never left the subject matter for personal asides either about herself or any of the students, she did not make jokes at the expense of the material or ever give any indication that grammar and punctuation were less than very important matters. She never compromised. And it worked. It was the best grammer lesson I had ever seen and it was particularly interesting because all of the students were bound up into it, just as she was. Students knew and volunteered the answers and looked as if they cared about them. When a student was wrong he or she acted as if it mattered. It was a good class and she was a good teacher, but there was one very interesting thing: The white and black students interacted easily with one another over the matter of the work. A white would turn around to exchange paper with and talk to blacks, and black students did the same to whites. That does sound like a fairly simple act but in Urban High it was a rarity, because it represented a truce between blacks and whites. I noticed at the end of the class the blacks went out with other blacks just as the whites went out with other whites, but during the period of the class they really were integrated.

There were other excellent classes like Mrs. S.'s, and excellent teachers. We watched them in philosophy, French, auto shop, welding, gymnastics, and computers. In the next chapter I want to examine the way these teachers discuss their own approach to their positions and why they bring quality into their classes. In that chapter we will explore the differences between Mrs. S., with her all-consuming approach to teaching English grammer, and Mr. P., about whom we were unclear just what it was he was doing in that school beyond picking up his check. But that will not contradict the major points made here; that in those schools each teacher was left alone and responsible for maintaining order in the classroom, and that the order seemed to emanate from personal relations with the students. While some people seem to make the good personal relations the end, and some use it as a means to instruction, both operate under the same set of organizational constraints. There are serious differences among teachers, to be sure, but differences between teachers are not the focus of this book as much as is the structure of the schools. For our purpose, the most interesting point about the differences between Mrs. S. in her grammar class and Mr. P. in his social studies class is that they both operate within the same organization and are both regarded as acceptable teachers. In other words, once a teacher proved that he could maintain order, neither the organization nor anyone speaking for the organization made any qualitative judgments about him or her.

One of the difficulties of comparing Mrs. S. and Mr. P. is that she did have a set of students who had elected a course known informally to be "college prep" and he did have a course that was known to be not college prep. That was probably part of it, but on the other hand, in that open elective system there was no guarantee that the courses informally known as college prep attracted only good students. There was nothing to prevent poorer students from entering those classes if they so chose. On the other hand, there was nothing to assure that the students in Mrs. P.'s class were poor students. There might have been a number in there who made a bad choice, who just did not feel like working, or who were there because of a scheduling problem. The remaining fact is that Mrs. S., for her own reasons, decided to teach school; Mr. P., for his own reasons, decided not to.

THE LIMITS OF STUDENT INTEREST

In the first few pages of the chapter I discussed the great diversity among the courses offered in each of the schools. There are a number of ways to justify creating myriad courses and letting the students chose among them, as did these schools, but the major one is that it represents an attempt to find something of interest to students. In all the schools we studied that was a major end of the teachers and the organization. As I saw most of the teachers in those schools, they were quite willing to stretch the definition of an education as long as they could get students interested in something. But that was often discouraging, as the cross country coach expressed one day when an hour before an after-school meet, one of his runners came to him and said: "I can't be there today."

"*You what!*" "I have to go take care of my grandmother who just got out of the hospital because my mom has to take my little sister to skating practice." The coach gave the student a lecture on what it meant to be an athlete and how if one of the five cross country runners did not show up the meet would be forfeited, as it already had been once that year, and sent the boy off with the order to "be there." The boy left, caught between his extended family and his coach. The coach then talked about how hard it was to get the students interested and how the attitude shown by that boy prevailed in the school. "One time they tried to raise money for a booster club for the school, we went out and sold hot dogs and pop and candy at the games, and when we had money we wanted to have a dinner for the athletes at the end of the year. But so few people came it was embarrassing. OK, so you don't want to have a dinner, we'll have a trip. So more preparation and only a few people came there. Then we tried a canoeing trip up north, and there were more coaches and helpers than kids. Finally, I gave that stuff up. I don't know what they want." Reflecting on it he attributed it to the fact that "these are the less affluent kids, we can't get them away from working and into school."

This business of kids more interested in working to support their car than school was widely cited in all the schools. Indeed, over two-thirds of the senior class in Suburban High left school after the fifth period to go to their jobs, and one half the junior class did the same. Teachers disparaged it and blamed it on two elements: the working-class environment in the community and the car that the student needed a job to sustain. "Hey, they get a license and then they get a car and then the old lady looks at that insurance check and says, I think it's time you got a job! Then work is the most important thing in their lives."

And indeed, for those who left that school early in the day to go to work, as did over half the juniors and seniors, that was certainly true. Despite the great increase in opportunities for elective classes, what the students elected first was to leave school as soon as they could and go to work. In that school not only did that have a major effect on the schedule and on the range of possible classes, but it was particularly discouraging to teachers who were interested in doing something for students, many of whom did not seem to want anything more than the minimum done for them.

It was stated earlier that there were 250 courses in one school and 168 courses in another. Curriculum enlargement represented an attempt to have the curriculum fit the students' needs. The issue of needs was never addressed directly; it seemed to be backed into. What happened was that students in many many classes were not particularly interested in "positive knowledge," but one cannot officially admit that because to do so would challenge the legitimacy of the institution. So, rather than admitting it, which would be disfunctional for the school and the larger society, schools embark on an endless search for elective subjects to attract and interest students. "Girl talk," "what's happening," "personal relations," "man-to-man," and "troubleshooter" were some of the electives that people created in English and social studies. Further, these schools had taken what were formerly school activities and sports and turned them into credit classes. One "took" yearbook, student council, newspaper, band, glee club, orchestra, debate, drama, swimming, life saving, golf, gymnastics, modern dance, ballet, stagecraft, chorale, or student government. Or one took a variety of aide positions in which one earned one-half credit for helping some teacher or working in the office, library, or audio-visual center. One took cooperative education in which the job that one acquired for the purpose of earning money was co-opted into the school curriculum and one was given credit for engaging in a "learning activity." The proliferation of courses such as these represents an attempt on the part of teachers to find something that the students would take, like, and work on. If they did that, then it was assumed that their "needs" were being met, and the role of the school was legitimized.

I am reminded of a conversation with the superintendent of a moderate-sized school district, also in the metropolitan area. He was recounting a story of a biology teacher in his system who cared little for biology but a great deal about hunting and fishing, and it was generally known that those latter topics, not biology, dominated his classes. With pride, the superintendent recounted how he and the principal had encouraged that teacher to drop biology and write up and offer an "outdoor education" elective. According to the superintendent, the teacher did that, and now his classes are all fully subscribed and the students are satisfied. "And that," concluded the superintendent, "is good for kids." Now just what it was that was "good for kids" was unclear to me, and when I asked it was apparent that it was equally unclear to the superintendent. School people have a way of passing this "good for kids" phrase off without any critical thought, but it seems to be a combination of the students getting what they sign up for (it did not matter what) and the teacher putting some emotion and energy into his classes. Of course there was never any attempt to address the issue of whether outdoor education was even worthwhile, let alone better than biology. That superintendent expressed perfectly just what I had seen in those high schools I studied. From the organizational perspective, it did not matter what was taught or even what was learned as long as there was some "liking of the kids" on the part of teachers and some "interest in something" on the part of students. And where the latter was absent, the former was sufficient to legitimize the effort. But even in the face of these efforts, the students in Factory High seemed content to leave school at 12:35 to go home or wherever they go, and the majority of juniors and seniors in Suburban High left as early as possible to go to their jobs. Again we have to consider the limits of the appeal of positive knowledge for many students. Despite the blandishments of the expanded curriculum and the academic credits given for participation in activities, for work experience or aide positions, the great majority of students, while civil and decently behaved, did not seem terribly interested in pursuing any topic beyond what was minimally required.

SUMMARY

In this chapter I tried to move beyond the halls and administrative offices into classrooms to explore the ways the internal and external constraints affect the curriculum. The conventional assumption would have it that the curriculum of a school exists as a body of knowledge, agreed upon by staff and approved by the general community and by district authorities who have some expertise, and that it reflects the best thinking about what young people need in order to succeed in our society. But I did not find that. Rather it seemed that constraints took over and the agreed-upon body of knowledge (if indeed there ever was one) got shunted aside in favor of maintaining order and appealing to students. Cordiality or "liking and getting along with kids" was more important than any agreed-upon body of knowledge.

One may use the cordiality to spend the entire period in small talk, as did Mr. P., or one may use it to as part of an aggressive teaching style, as did Mrs. S. What is interesting is that both of these accommodations are equally acceptable because each satisfies the major constraint, that the school take everyone and maintain order.

Consider the position of a teacher faced with a set of students, many of whom have a history of nonachievement. They may be perfectly decent adolescents, quite open to good relations with teachers and peers, but with little interest in literature, history, mathematics, science or world affairs, or auto mechanics. One has to "survive" for the period with these students who give so much evidence of so little interest in the acquisition of positive knowledge. The way one does that is build some decent relations with the students, which not only helps to keep them in a state of moderate order but satisfies the administrators' desire for teachers who "like kids" and who do not send kids to the office. And those good relations, rather than the agreed-upon and approved body of knowledge, become the real genesis of curriculum. According to the model I am developing, that accommodation to the problematic elements inherent in the school is the key element to understanding the structure of these three and perhaps other secondary schools.

NOTES

1. North Central Association of Colleges and Schools, *Policies and Standards for the Approval of Secondary Schools* (Boulder, Colo.: NCACS, 1979–80), p. 16.

4

The Curriculum, Part II

INTRODUCTION

Chapter 2 gave an explanation of the major constraints on the schools studied, the obligation to take and provide some sort of instruction for everyone and at the same time maintain an orderly atmosphere. These two constraints could work against each other. Maintaining an orderly atmosphere was not easy when schools had to accommodate a number of students who were not particularly interested in receiving instruction, or in the case of the biracial schools, had some strong antagonisms toward one another. When these two major constraints came into conflict, taking everyone and maintaining order preempted providing instruction. That is a hard conclusion, but it is the only way to explain the fact that some few teachers did little or no instructing yet maintained their positions because they could "get along with the kids."

One might simply say that there are different kinds of teachers just as there are different kinds of people in every profession. But that does not explain why such different types of accommodations were equally acceptable and equally rewarded within the same school, or why there were no attempts on the part of anyone to get those who were doing nothing to do something. Part of the answer lies with the fact that supervisory and administrative time was taken up with attendance, discipline, and public relations. But there are other ways to encourage effort and compliance without resorting to a hierarchial authority. One can conceive of an organization wherein the staff holds some common expectations of one another and those commonly held norms serve to stimulate effort. Such mechanisms did not exist in any of the schools I studied. There were norms to be sure, but a major one was that no teacher interfered with the way another conducted his or her classes. Therefore the individual teacher was allowed the freedom to work out his or her own curriculum and approach to instruction.

The argument runs thus. The first and only real obligation of the teachers is to maintain order and discipline, and the way each does that is through the sustaining of cordial relations with the students. At base each wants and is expected to "like and get along with the kids." Those good personal relations emanate not from some agreed-upon school curriculum but rather from the kind of person each teacher is. What will be elaborated upon in this chapter is that just as the maintenance of good relations emanates from the kind of person each individual is, so one's instructional style and the content one emphasizes also emanates from the kind of person one is. Just as one is free to get along with the students the way he or she sees fit, one is also free to decide on his or her own approach to curriculum and teaching. In Chapter 3 I outlined the extensive curriculum in two of those comprehensive high schools, but here I will argue that the outlines do not begin to reveal the actual breadth of the curriculum because they do not take into account the teachers' idiosyncratic approaches. One of the studies was of the "network" of interactions among the faculties of two schools, Factory High and Suburban High. I wanted to know, What is taught and how do teachers, singly or together, work out an agreement on what is taught?

CREATING CURRICULUM

The sixty-eight teachers in Suburban High had similar backgrounds. Almost every one of them had come from that same metropolitan area, had attended one or more of the same three nearby state colleges for undergraduate and graduate work, and had been with that school district for all of their teaching years. There were exceptions. One recounted how he had been a factory worker, active in the local labor movement, had later gone into farming and after running himself $20,000 into debt, accepted the advice of the local banker and went to teach school to pay his debts. Others had moved out from the central part of the metropolitan area; some of them had known each other since childhood. But almost none were from another part of the country, or even the state, or had attended colleges other than those three that were nearby. The hiring process was a bit casual. A teacher was hired because he or she graduated with a major in some needed specialty, knew someone, or was connected somehow in the district and was available. No one reported being recruited because of his or her record, nor wanting to come to the district for some reason other than geographical, that is, it was "near home." No one accounted for his position because of scholarship, a winning record or dedication, nor did anyone report himself to have brought in some unusual specialty. Since most of them came right from undergraduate school, that expectation might have been unrealistic. But on the other hand no one reported that she or he was trying to build an outstanding record which would convert to a better job. When possible the administrators hired those who were related to or who knew local people as a means to further cementing the already good community relations. The district wanted a shop, physical education, or English teacher, and if someone had the certificate and degree and seemed all right, then fine. If someone had the certificate and the degree and seemed all right, and was known to people in the school or the community, then all the better. Someone who was known was always preferable to a stranger.

Factory High had one hundred and one teachers with a variety of backgrounds. It had been a district policy in the 1960s to recruit black teachers, and a number of them had come from schools in the South. In addition to being from other parts of the country, many had experience other than teaching. A few had been in the ministry or business, some had been administrators in other districts, and two had been professional athletes.

In both districts, which were only minutes apart on a state four-lane highway, teachers had little interest in the communities other than their employment in the schools. There really was little to either of the communities. Factory High was adjacent to the city's downtown area, which consisted only of a few civic buildings, a railroad crossing, and an intersection of two state highways. Stores, businesses, and pedestrians had left for the suburbs some years ago. In the suburban area there was also a downtown, but it consisted of only a few gas stations, bars, a few stores, and a travel agency. It had been a farming village before the influx of people moving out from the central city, but the town itself had not changed much except for the increased traffic that passed by on the main road.

On the other hand, for many, the school district itself contained important social ties. Many teachers had been in their respective buildings for years and had developed friendships with other teachers in the district while working on committees or in student activities. Many had spouses working for the same district in other schools. In the suburban area, many were children of or were somehow related to other district employees. In both districts, many of the coaches and administrators took a very lively interest in the fortunes of their own school's teams and in teams from other district high schools. The administrators of both buildings had transferred around the district and were well acquainted with administrators in other buildings. In the suburban district, some teachers from the district regularly made a spring trip together. There were many connecting friendships and social relations of all types that had been going on for years.

The study I made was of curriculum development. The central concept was network and the orienting questions: How do people create curriculum through and out of their involvement with one another and with various aspects of the school and community? More specifically, I asked the staffs, individually and collectively, "What do you do in class, and how do you decide on what you do?" If one asked a superintendent or assistant principal for curriculum that question, one would be given the board's curriculum manual, accrediting agency guidelines, state requirements, course and sequence listings, and graduation requirements. All that was duly collected and studied, but it did not begin to describe the complex curricula of those schools nor did it give any hints as to the origin of those curricula.

Two generalizations may be made. First, the structure of the schools provided a great deal of freedom to individual teachers. There were bounds, to be sure. One had to arrive at a specific time and might not leave before another specific time. One was also bound to teach five classes; in Suburban High there was an additional duty assignment, and in both districts the teachers had to attend a few teachers' meetings a year. And in Suburban High the contract demanded that they attend two after-hours school events each year. But in neither school was the teachers' contract much more specific than that regarding the way they were to conduct themselves in or out of class. Second, the teachers accepted those bounds and then proceeded to create a curriculum that suited themselves within those limits. One was free to find his or her own way to teach, a way which fit his or her individual style, and then justify it in terms of it being "good for kids." Some stressed reading and writing, some personal relations, some deportment. Some assigned homework, some did not; some spoke to students in the teenage jargon and themselves behaved as teenagers; some held up adult standards of speech and behavior. Some put normative compliance into their jobs and made them the center of their lives. Others gave little time and put their involvement into their families, second jobs, or avocations. There was no standard curriculum nor any standard way to behave relative to the curriculum.

Part of this can be attributed to the electiveness of the curriculum, an element that has been in secondary schools for many years. It is integrally bound up with the major constraints about taking everyone and the basic assumption about the acquisition of positive knowledge. Since the schools have to take and provide something for everyone, they are constantly casting about for ways to interest their students. The basic response to the demand is the elective system, which permits the curriculum to be expanded according to either internal or external constraints, and further allows standard requirements (e.g., one or two years of English) to be satisfied in a number of different ways. This organizational characteristic enables school people to demonstrate they are working to find different ways to satisfy the very different individuals who show up at the door, and also being responsive to this or that group which wants a particular specialty interjected into the curriculum.

Most of the major criticisms of schools for a number of years have been phrased in terms of their being too restrictive, unimaginative, or confining, and the response of the schools to such criticism is to use this electiveness to interject another set of offerings for some heretofore unheeded subset of the population. So, not only does the characteristic of electiveness give public evidence of serving the needs of all the students, it solves the practical problem of providing an answer to public criticisms. On the other hand, this electiveness has some costs. For one, it means that teachers have to compete with one another for students to fill their classes. It can and did happen in the schools I studied that there were some good and demanding teachers who did not have enough students to teach. This may force teachers to heighten the emphasis on maintaining the good relations with students and deemphasize a relationship based on some common interest in the subject matter. A second, and more serious effect, is that since electivenesses is accompanied by an open, nontracked system, a student is faced with this expanded curriculum and left largely on his own to decide which of the eighteen, nineteen, or twenty he will take for his high school education. That may not be a totally negative effect. There are high school students who are either very mature or who have sufficient parental guidance to help them make their choices. But for those who are neither mature nor receiving any parental guidance, such a system may not be beneficial. In fact, such a system may further disadvantage the already disadvantaged.

A third, possibly negative, effect is the proliferation of courses, the sum of which makes little sense. Hence those who speak for the school may and do have a hard time explaining just what the curriculum is all about and how it fits the goals of the school. When administrators explain what schools are all about, they do so in terms of satisfying the "needs of kids." But with the needs left undefined, as they always are, it seems that the schools range about to find something teachers will teach and to which students will respond, and upon finding it proclaim it as meeting the students' "educational needs."

While this seems curious, it does have a functional logic, and it seems to describe what happened in the schools I studied. As a characteristic, electiveness is deeply embedded in the structure of our schools, so much so that if one were to question it, one would have to consider the nature of the total school. Since that is the subject of this book, this chapter will center around the way that teachers in the subject schools created the curriculum.

A long-time teacher in Factory High created an English elective in philosophy and gradually built it up by recruiting students to the point where he had three classes each term, all well subscribed. The philosophy he taught was Aristotle, because that was what interested him, but he could have taught Hume and Berkeley and it would have been equally acceptable because no one ever questioned him. He had a strong church background, having been a seminarian in a Catholic order, read philosophy in his spare time, taught it at the community college, and when asked why he created a course in philosophy replied in terms of "the unexamined life not being worth living." This is true enough, and it is also true that the belief came from his own background, education, religion, and personal preferences, all of which combined to support what he did in the classroom.

A social studies teacher who had served in and was a student of World War II, started a war games club and used the proceeds from candy sales to buy some elaborate games. He enlarged the club into an elective class and recruited students from the club for the class. He then worked it up to three classes of a social studies elective called "World War II."

A French teacher in Suburban High took over French III when it had three students and with energy and hard work built it up to twenty-three students. This was a noteworthy accomplishment in advanced foreign language class in a school where the teachers generally considered the kids to be "working class and blue collar." Every year she took as many as would go to Quebec, every other year as many as would go to Paris; her French Club had dinners where only French was spoken, and she took the students to ethnic restaurants in the metropolitan area. She spent her spare time reading and studying for her classes. "Why do you do all that?" "Because I want to make French an exciting subject; I want the kids to say, 'Hey, French is a good subject to take; it's fun and exciting.' I want it to be the best class in the school. When it's a conflict between home and job, my husband stays home and I come to school. If I have to be here at night, he comes with me and we bring the kids. My job comes first in our family." "Why do you do that?" "Because I want to make French class an exciting place . . . I want them to love French," and so forth. Always when I posed the question "why" to these teachers, who by their own account and the account of others gave a great deal to the school, I found the particulars of their approach came from their own background, personal interests, hobbies, families, and the like; the "why" came from their own desire to put all of that together in the classroom.

Whenever we talked to people who worked hard at teaching we always asked about the reward they received for their time and energy. They did it "for the kids," "for the satisfaction," for the pleasure, because "that's the kind of person I am," because "I like it." The answers were always phrased in terms of personal relationships with students. The head of the athletic department in Factory High opened the gym to students whenever he could, availed himself to students after hours, bought his wrestlers' meals from his own pocket during trips, and worked in the gym on weekends and evenings for little or no money, just "to keep it open for kids." He recounted his own childhood in a poor Polish section of Chicago. He spoke of how hard the 1930s were, when he was in his childhood; what sports had done for him, and how otherwise he never would have gone to a major university nor would he have graduated if he had gone. He saw his students as needing the same kind of guidance that participation in sports brought to him.

The biology teacher in Suburban High lived on a lake, was the state president of Ducks Unlimited and influential with people in the Department of Natural Resources. He hunted and fished all the time, often with students and former students, and took his interests in forests and streams into the classroom. When asked why he gave such enthusiasm to the classroom, he replied, "When it gets to be a job, then I quit. I was an embalmer, and a machinist, and a shop man, and this is the first job I ever had where I really like to go to work. I never get up and wish I didn't have to go in. Sometimes I feel bad in the morning, but when I get here it goes away. I hated teaching junior high school, but here a kid can be a human being and be related to." At this point he proudly showed me a letter from a student who had left the previous year but just wrote back from college to tell him about some work in biology he was doing. Everything came together for him: his graduate work in biology, avocations, public service, teaching, and liking of adolescents. His main life interests all meshed into his teaching. To the question, "Why do you do what you do in the classroom and take the approach you take," he would verbally construct this egocentric field where teaching as he taught was extended from and intertwined with a host of other elements in his life.

It was not that these people were merely expressing their beliefs, predilections, and approach to education. Their classroom behavior, the subject matter they stressed, and the way they related to students followed those idiosyncratic elements. A highly regarded English teacher in Urban High had for some years made speech his specialty. He worked with the debate club, which had established a very creditable record, and also taught forensics. His speech classes were particularly interesting. Students were asked to give three or four speeches a term, one on their personal lives, one on their aspirations, and two on other topics, but the teacher was most proud that, in the more difficult classes, with his encouragement students got up and talked in detail about the sordid aspects of their lives. Any time one encourages the telling of real-life situations from poor students in urban schools, he can bring forth some dreadful events. "Yesterday this little white girl got up and talked about a man she was baby sitting for and how he raped her repeatedly over a period of six weeks. And you should have seen those black guys respond to her and tell her that if she would point him out they would 'fix his ass for good.'" The next day I attended a class and found a small white girl relating a tale of being thrown out of her house by her stepfather, and how a black neighbor had taken her in and now she was feeling better about herself in particular and black people in general. While this waif was relating her tale about the wicked stepfather, the teacher sat in the back of the room and threw in the leading questions: "And what did you feel when that happened?" "How did those people respond when they found out what you went through?" "How do you feel about that now that you look back on it?" The girl built her speech around her answers to the questions. He tried to bring in others among the fourteen students, but each seemed to have pulled into him or herself, half-watching, half-listening with no commitment to the event related. When the teacher spoke of his efforts to teach "this English elective for kids who can't read," he spoke glowingly of their openness with one another, of the affection that came through to one who had told of his or her plight, of how his elective was one of the best-subscribed classes in the school. He was proud of the fact that while he was white, his students were almost all black, "except for a few strong whites." And when he spoke to them of their experiences he used a street argot, referring to their "ladies," the pimping and prostitution, drugs, welfare. When I asked: "Why do you do this?" his response was an expression of his personal assessment of the students: "This is what they need. They need someone who understands where they're coming from and who can talk to them. This is the way to relate to these kids, this is where they're at in their lives and if you want to relate to them, this is the way to do it." It was not the same response given by the French teacher or philosophy teacher or World War II teacher, but it was the same type of response in that it emanated from the teacher's personal assessment, interests, and predilections.

This teacher was highly regarded by administrators, worked very hard with his debate team, cared about the students, and had created this approach to curriculum based on his personal assessment of the students and the situation, but one could legitimately ask if students in an elective English class really need what it was he was teaching. Perhaps. Perhaps not. What was interesting was that there was no mechanism in the structure to even ask, let alone answer, the question. Any teacher in those schools was free to make his assessment, create and carry through his classes using a combination of his own beliefs, values, and perspective as his referent. This gentleman was proud of his success at getting students to articulate their lives, particularly the seamier side, and empathize with their peers, particularly members of the "other" race.

There were a number of interesting elements in this teacher's approach, and one of them was that he spoke of the "enthusiasm of the kids" for what he was doing. But I could not see that enthusiasm. Rather, I saw him adding the enthusiasm and then pretending the student had done it. A boy was giving a speech on his aspirations, but it was really a set of disorganized ramblings. "Well, I wanna open a clothing store you know, I like clothes and I like to dress up, it's important you know, and . . ." The teacher was in the back of the room prodding the student. "Does your interest in clothes make you want to do this?" "Yeah, that's it," said the student, and went on about the type of clothes. "Do you think clothes are important to a person?" "Well, yeah, you know, when a guy looks good that's important . . ." and the student went on, interrupted again by the teacher asking if his ambition was to make a lot of money. The student responded again, "Well, yeah, you know," and went on briefly. It took only a few minutes. There was no outline, no preparation, and what structure it had came from the teacher coaxing the student into following an outline that he, not the student, had in front of him. In that "English elective for the kids who can't read" (as he put it) that was how the teacher created speeches for the students to give, and in the process made the personal relations between he and them, and among blacks and whites, the real subject matter.

But, as with other teachers who worked hard to find ways to establish and maintain affective relations with low-achieving students, the burden seemed to be entirely on him. We were talking in the hall one day, and as a boy passed the teacher took him by the arm and said, "Hey, I want to thank you for that presentation yesterday, it was just terrific." "Uhhh, yeah, sure," said the boy, turning back to his friend and carrying on their conversation, which the teacher had interrupted. The teacher then explained enthusiastically the project the boy had completed, but it seemed to me that just as in class that teacher was bearing the burden of the relationship. Neither that student nor the ones in class appeared to be giving much. They were respectful and decently behaved, but much less involved than the teacher's words indicated. That limited interest compels individual teachers into ranging about to find something to interest and involve students. It seemed to me that frequently the burden of demonstrating some interest and involvement lay with the teachers. What could the teacher do? He admitted that the students could barely read. Could he also admit that many of them did not care? Were he to do that he might be faced with the futility of the whole endeavor and himself become discouraged. His answer was if they cannot read, find something worthwhile that they can do; and if they seemed to care little, then he would add that caring. I could see why, despite his unorthodox approach, he was regarded as successful.

For this analysis, the most important point about these schools is that having no way of addressing what the students might "need," yet having to demonstrate that the students' needs were being met, the obligation came down to each individual teacher. Accompanying that obligation was the freedom to create and sustain and justify his or her classes in the way each chose. In effect each was free to take his own set of values and predilections, the genesis of which can only be guessed at, and from that assemble his or her approach to teaching, justifying whatever the result as being "good for kids." It is as a teacher who spent a great deal of time and energy organizing a benefit for a girl stricken with a kidney disease said, in response to some criticism from teachers who said it was a waste of time, "If that isn't what we're here for, I don't know what is." Whatever a teacher decided to do, he or she always justified it just like that, with simple statements of belief about what was good for students.

A particular English teacher in that urban school who loved music put on musical performances and worked as a show promoter for some local agencies. He created an English elective called "Music as Expression," where he played the Beatles, street rock, the Beach Boys and all the music he liked in classes that were quite well subscribed by both blacks and whites. The program consisted of listening to the music, then studying and writing about the lyrics. He referred to his class as "relevant" and "interesting" and was very proud of having the "most popular elective class in this school." Among other pieces he presented were the street poet Gill Scott Herron's "Niggers Love to Say F—" and "When the Revolution Comes."

Other English teachers might and some did disparage what "he calls English," but according to him, "This is what those kids relate to and if you're going to relate to them it has to be on these terms. You have to talk their language." And indeed, his classes were orderly, he was pre-pared, students were civil, the gamier handouts (such as those by Herron) were collected at the end of class so that no one would be passing the lyrics around the school. Overall he was a careful and conscientious teacher.

But so was the social studies teacher down the hall, who insisted that the students memorize the pramble to the United States Constitution, that they learn the "Pledge of Allegiance, even if they can't spell it," that they study and understand the Bill of Rights, and that they salute the flag at the beginning of class (the latter a simply unheard-of event in either school); and he assigned and demanded homework. He believed in "teach-ing something to them; they don't know anything about their country and they don't have any appreciation; all they know how to do is shout some empty slogan that they heard somewhere and that they don't begin to understand, and that passes for knowing something. I won't let that hap-pen in my classes." He also took a hard physical line toward students, something that I had not seen in a long time. "I tell them in the beginning, if you don't like me and you want to take a swing then do it, but make it a good one because it will be the only one you get."

He was one of the few teachers who spoke contemptously about con-ditions in the school, about students running the halls, the lack of standards of dress and language, the general lack of discipline. "If any teacher gets hurt here and he gets a smart lawyer, he'll be able to retire rich because it will come out in public just what's allowed to go on here." We discussed the fact that what other teachers saw as a realistic accommodation to the students as they were, he saw as an "inexcusable lessening of standards." He was also the only white teacher who talked openly of race problems in the schools. "Hell, everybody knows it's the black kids running up and down the halls and beating up the white kids. The white kids aren't beating up the black kids. But everybody's afraid to do anything about it. They're even afraid to say it."

But it was not just a matter of some teachers accommodatiing the students by discarding standards, some maintaining their allegiance to the material and sustaining standards. High school staffs are frequently dicho-tomized into the "kid oriented" and the "subject oriented" teachers. But no one saw himself or herself in such simple terms, nor is it fair to present anyone that way. Each teacher's approach was a reflection of his back-ground, values, and predilections, and the approaches were as complex as the mix of elements. At times, I would try to trace with a particular teacher his or her approach with questions such as: "Why do you want them to memorize the preamble to the Constitution?" but it never worked. There are certainly very good reasons for doing that, and all one had to do was call on the one that was most available, "Because they have to understand their country. They're Americans, aren't they?" Of course they are and of course it was a reasonable assignment for a teacher to make. I got nowhere when I tried to be analytical about such straightforward statements of belief. Teachers never bothered to equivocate about alternative approaches. Theirs was such a part of them that they did not seem to consider another. I was never successful in my attempts to trace these bits of curriculum back through the teacher's idiosyncracies and predilections. But then I was not trying to analyze individuals. I was trying to understand and describe the structure of these comprehensive secondary schools. As I understood the curriculum, it included whole ranges of things that teachers dredged from their own lives, any and all of which were justified by the simple statement, "It's good for the kids."

There was an important point in this phrase "good for kids" because each teacher had a specific set of students for whom his approach was good. It was not just an abstracted or generalized "kids" for whom the particular approach worked. It was always specific students. Of course there were those in both schools who disparaged the general levels of students. "I ask them for a current event and they tell me Farrah is no longer on 'Charlie's Angels.' For them that's a current event." But even those teachers had a few students whom they felt joined in on an affective level. The speech teacher had this "little white girl," a special education teacher had a few "former students, friends of mine today, and they just disappeared into the community and no one remembers they were special." Another had some scholarship students, another, former students. Mr. L. never forgot: "When I was talking about the Romans sending 40,000 troops into Gaul in the summer of 9 A.D., Bob Sullivan raised his hand and said, 'Mr. L., I think you're wrong, it must have been spring of 9 A.D., because the calendar we have is three months different from the calendar we had then.'"

The student referent was different for each teacher. Earlier, I mentioned a boy named Luther who had hit the principal from behind and later was sent to prison for rape and abduction. Some teachers detested him, but the creative writing teacher found him to be a sensitive and intelligent student who "responded well to praise, when he came in here he had only one kid he related to and that was another street kid like himself. It took them a whole term to establish themselves in the class. They looked around a lot, but he worked well . . . he wrote some sensitive lines."

A wrestling coach/biology teacher at Suburban High had "this one kid, all of his brothers dropped out of school, then his sister was dropping out and his parents didn't care, but I got ahold of him, kept him wrestling for me, and he's still in school and going to graduate. I tell him to stay in school and try to graduate, I work with him, try to get him to do better, I talk to him and encourage him. Now the other teachers come to me when they have a problem with him and I take care of it."

In some ways one may be critical of this phrase "good for kids" because of the license it allowed teachers to do anything they felt like doing in the class. But I was always impressed by the genuine affection with which teachers spoke of the few students with whom they had a personal relation and whom they then used as their justifying referent, and I was equally impressed by how far they would go to help those who were responsive. In all the schools the student body was sufficiently diverse so that a teacher could find a few who would respond. Just as there was no consensus on what was good for kids, neither was there any on which kids something was good for. Teachers could not cut themselves off from those who did not give any kind of response, but they could and (it seemed to me) did treat those students perfunctorily while holding out that hope for and promise of affective relations with those who would join in their endeavor.

The phrase "good for kids" was neatly holistic. It included the teacher's own values, beliefs, interests, and predilections whence developed his or her approach to teaching; it included the approach itself, and it always included a set of "kids" for whom the approach had worked or was presently working. In such a system one did not need the support of his fellow teachers. One had his style, students, unsupervised isolation, and was therefore reasonably free to create his courses, find those students who responded, and justify his endeavor with reference to them.

It may appear that I have been critical of the quality of these schools, but I do not mean to do that. In both were many excellent teachers running what I thought were very high-quality classes. But what was interesting in this study of structure, was that quality was not something that either school as an institution was capable of addressing. Rather, it was left to individual teachers to define and offer it as they wished and to individual students to define and seek it out if they wished. No teacher would admit to offering less than quality classes, and since students seldom talk in those terms, the issue was left unaddressed. If the students were in attendance (which most were) and orderly in class (which most were), and if the teachers appeared to like and get along with their students (which most did), then the important things were being attended to. If some teacher wanted to stress what he called "quality" and could do it within the major constraint (getting along with kids), then he was free to do so. And if some student wanted a particular sort of "quality" education, then he was free to define and ferret it out. In all cases, the matter of defining and delivering quality was left to the individual.

I may have gone too far in stressing the uniqueness of each teacher's approach. Both schools had an "established" curriculum and both had a set of procedures for altering that curriculum. Factory High had an assistant principal for curriculum, and if one wanted to initiate a new course, then he went to that person with the idea and further developed the course with the person's cooperation. In Suburban High there was a school department structure, a system-wide department structure, and a curriculum committee run by the director of secondary education. A new offering, a change in texts, or the removal of a course went through a process that took some months and received careful scrutiny, particularly from the system-wide curriculum committee. And each school was allocated a certain number of teachers based on the number of students. Given the standard curriculum, it was then the principal's task in Suburban High or the assistant principal's in Factory High to schedule the curriculum with what staff was available. These procedures were fairly orderly, and from my observations were well followed in both places.

However, even with these formal procedures, the point still stands. While the curricula in either school were referred to as "standard," there was really nothing standard about them. Each was the sum of what individual teachers had added over the years. What was published and advertised gave no hint as to what went on in class.

That the "curriculum" stands published does not mean that there was some system-wide rationale or even school-wide collective understanding of its appropriateness. Any change or innovation still came from individuals following their own predilections. The energy that altered the curriculum was always generated from one person, not allocated by the structure. Neither the assistant principal for curriculum nor the curriculum committee took the initiative in change. Given the absence of supervision or coordination, once a course was entered in, years could go by and no one in any position of authority ever asked, "What is happening in that class?" With that kind of system, even with the appearance of some rationality and coordination, there was much more diversity and disparity than was ever admitted. To understand the curriculum of a comprehensive high school, one has to understand these pressures that accompany electiveness. A contributing element is that in an elective system, the courses that are most offered are those that are most elected. A young teacher was hired into Suburban High to teach one class of physical science and four classes of chemistry. But he liked physical science better and also preferred the type of lower-achieving students who were likely to elect physical science. So he recruited more students into the physical science class, had to offer more sections, and soon was teaching four classes of physical science and one of chemistry.

Part of the source of the diversity can be traced to the absence in either school of any uniform opinion of students, who they are or what they need or what they best respond to. And part of it can be attributed to the schools' comprehensiveness, which justified placing all kinds of students under the same roof. In effect one could justify anything. Teachers could not only do what they wanted in class; they could also develop their own style of behavior. One physical education teacher was convinced that her hanging out with the students, use of scatological terms in addressing them, her less than casual attire, and her nonassertive approach to teaching (it was hard to tell who was the teacher in her classes) all combined according to her into the "best way to get along with the kids." And if one asked why she did all of that, she could justify her approach: "These teachers who dress up and make the kids talk just so and keep their distance from them, to me that's just phony, you have to be yourself with the kids." Her style was privately disparaged by a number of others, including the department chairman, but since the system had no mechanism to address the question of what was really "good for kids" nor any collective understanding of some goals and methods, she was free to do her job the way she saw fit. If someone had told her (no one ever did) that she was less than adequate, she would have recited her involvement in student activities, her initiating of girls' sports of all kinds, and the number of times she gave her personal assistance to troubled students. She had no trouble justifying her job and did not need the approval of other teachers, only particular students. Nor did the teacher who had the students reading street poetry, nor did the teacher who made them recount their personal lives, nor did anyone else ever have to subject his or her choice of content and behavior to some general school norms. The schools were not structured that way. And were they structured that way, they might not have been able to accommodate their major constraint, to take and provide some sort of education for everyone.

This is the reason why I extended the purpose of the study from examining the way teachers joined together to create curriculum to examining the way the curriculum extended from and was intertwined with the individual teachers' lives. The problem with asking only the first question was that an answer depended on there being some interactions and working of the curriculum through these interactions; but issues or events did not work their way through the faculty, not issues that were curricular or programmatic. The sum of the forces discussed, the lack of supervision or, one might better say, the taking up of supervisory time with student discipline, the weakness of departments, the isolation of teachers in the classroom, the lack of common values among teachers regarding student behavior, achievement, biracialism, appropriate educational goals, or what was "good for kids," all combined to prevent consensus. Yet no force served to build consensus. To build consensus would have required purposeful activity, teacher recruitment with consensus in mind, a great deal of time and effort given to common activities, perhaps a less diverse environment, a more homogeneous set of students, and some active supervision of the curriculum, none of which was available. So the teacher was free to go off, build his own approach to classes and curriculum, his own way of relating to students, and was then free to justify it in his own terms.

That the schools looked uniform was a function of the schedule, the room arrangement, and the requirements that one take some sequence of courses. But underneath that very thing uniformity was a great amount of diversity. Correspondingly, there was no mechanism to create uniformity out of the diversity. It was stated perfectly one day by Pat, a business teacher, when at lunch we were talking about this and he said, "It's like this, Phil, everybody subcontracts." He was right. Everybody does.

As open as the structure was, there were some limits, and explaining the limits has to do with extending the explanation of how the curriculum changes. One could do what one wished, but that some did more required others to do less. There were a limited number of periods in a day, there was competition among teachers for the time and interests of the better students, and there was limited money and resources. So while one could take an approach that he deemed fit given his predilections, there were some constraints which required the adoption of what might be called the entrepreneurial approach.

A particular teacher at Factory High had been hired to teach business math, but he was more interested in computers. He first started a computer club and interested a few students, who then took up selling candy and flowers to buy a few small computers. With these few he opened an elective class in computers. and recruited from his club enough students to keep it open. More candy sales, more computers, an arrangement with the central office to use their keypunch machines, and on occasion, their large computer, another arrangement with the intermediate district for access to some of their hardware as well as some financial help with software—and there were an additional two sections of the class. Operating like this over a period of three years, this teacher created a very credible introduction to programming and computer usage in that school, while at the same time he was deserting the business math classes for which he was hired.

This entrepreneurial approach was quite common in either school and accounted for the endless number of candy, flower, bake, bagel, and tee shirt sales. When I first entered those schools, I wondered why there were so many of those, but I found that behind each one there was a teacher who was raising funds to build up a particular elective class or activity.

There was also in that school an English teacher who, as the newspaper sponsor, decided to make journalism the center of her professional life. The $800 annual budget was not sufficient to put out the kind of quality newspaper she wanted, so she used the students in the journalism club to raise an extra $200 to $400 a month through candy, flower, and bake sales; she also recruited students for two additional classes in journalism. She found her own printer and borrowed a typesetting machine from the central office. Since the machine was off the maintenance list, she learned to do her own repairs. She also used her own funds to attend journalism seminars and took some students to these seminars. She wrote a proposal to the State Department of Education to support a job as districtwide journalism coordinator, a job she hoped to fill. Her newspaper was excellent, even though along the way she irritated the principal with her constant badgering for extra funds ("She wants to put out the *Washington Post* up there") and also some of the other English teachers, who felt she should stay closer to her English classes. But she had the impetus, and the entrepreneurial system favored those with the impetus.

The yearbook teacher in Suburban High was initially assigned one elective class of yearbook, but campaigned for and received a second, her case being that she needed to groom the juniors and sophomores into thinking about and assisting with the project before being given responsibility. She solicited the support of the vice principal for selection of the photographer she wanted, she carried on a number of candy and flower sales to keep the cost of the book to what the students could afford, and she recruited another teacher to teach a course in photography which she encouraged her students to take. Soon she had her whole job centered around her yearbook. As always, I asked why, and her idiosyncratic answer was phrased in terms of "giving the kids what they need. When I was in school, I was editor and it was the one think I liked best, and I wanted to do it here for these kids. That's the kind of person I am, I just can't do half a job. If we're going to have a yearbook, it's going to be the best in the state."

What was particularly interesting about the entrepreneurial approach was when one began there was no mechanism in the system for stopping him or her, not even by the administrators. An English teacher in Factory High over the years became discouraged at the reading level of his students and decided to become a remedial reading teacher. So he created a paperback library. He obtained $4,000 from the district and with his connections to a major book distributor used it to purchase $10,000 worth of paperbacks. He talked the principal into giving him a double classroom so he had one part to instruct and one to house the books. The content of his English classes became the individual readings. When the vice principal for curriculum told him to "get out of the library business" he simply ignored him and went on doing what he was doing. When the fire marshal complained about the stored books, he ignored him also. He even worked it out so that his "reading room," which started out as a separate activity or library, became a credit class. In response to the question "why" he gave a very reasonable and predictable answer. "That's what they need. They can't read. Here they learn to sit down in a quiet place and read a book; you think these kids get a quiet place at home? . . . And besides, the library is too formal for them." Other teachers laughed at his efforts: "He just did that to get a room [the reading room] to smoke in because he chain smokes and they wouldn't let him smoke in his classroom." But their opinions did not matter any more than the opinion of the vice principal. His school world consisted of his library, his connections, and his students, and he maintained it all by himself.

I have argued that one may do what he wishes in the classroom, but the more complex undertakings that demand extra effort or resources require one to enter a larger arena and engage in the necessary maintenance activities, such as fund raising, politicizing, and co-opting people who command needed resources. A logical question arises here: What about the department structure? It would seem that a departmental structure in which decisions about content were made would mitigate against the kind of activities I have described. To the degree that I could, I followed that issue, but I was limited in both of those schools because I just could not find departments doing much as departments. The English Department of Suburban High was composed of people who maintained very decent and cordial relations with one another; some were close personal friends, and in the course of continuing their jobs worked out class schedules, texts, supplies, and other matters. But, in the year of the study, there was only one event which demanded some extended cooperation, and I watched it because it was the only of its kind I encountered.

Two years prior to the study, the district had adopted a system-wide program in English to coordinate language arts across the district's four secondary schools. The effort had been initiated by two secondary English teachers who wanted to see more system-side emphasis on "basis skills," as well as a more coordinated program. With the approval of the superintendent, they called a meeting of all the secondary English teachers in the district, explained what they had in mind, and began by asking those teachers to make public what they were doing in their classes by handing in their course outlines. But according to the former system-wide chairman, "They [the teachers] just sat there with their arms folded and said in effect, 'You can't make me do anything,' and eventually the superintendent himself had to come in and tell them to hand in their outlines." "And did they do it then?" "No, not even then, they still sat there, but the truth, and we knew it, was that many of them didn't even have course outlines." Eventually the originators found some people in each school who would help develop and gather course outlines. In the school I studied, the department chairman told the two originators that "our people don't even have these things, so Gail (another teacher) and I did them all. For weeks we worked on them from seven in the morning until twelve at night, and she was pregnant and sometimes she would have to leave, and I'd be there typing until midnight." Eventually they handed in all the English outlines from all the courses taught in the school. Whether teachers in the other school compiled them in the same way I do not know, but the outlines were handed in and a summary of the district's total English curriculum compiled. Then a meeting of all the English teachers was held, and they approved the general curriculum and sent it to the Board of

Education, which also approved. Apparently what they approved system-wide (although there were varying versions of this) was a greater emphasis on basic skills with some systematic pre- and posttesting.

In the school I studied, the former chairman of the department had taken this very seriously, had written the grammar lessons herself, had written the pre- and posttests that were to be stressed in freshman and sophomore classes, developed scoring sheets to accompany the tests, distributed tests herself to make sure it was done correctly, and kept elaborate testing files locked in the department office. Having at least the passive cooperation of the whole department, she was herself doing what was supposed to be done in each of the other three schools, as well as what was supposed to be being done by the individual teachers. But in two of the other high schools, no similar efforts were being made. The outlines were compiled and ignored.

A second point that took some asking around to discover was that, despite the considerable amount of time and effort the chairman and some other members of the department had expended, no one, not the principal nor any assistant, nor the director of secondary education in the district, nor the superintendent, nor the board, nor anyone outside the department ever looked at the tests, commented on the system for testing and record keeping, or even acknowledged the change. In fact, the director of secondary education did not even mention to the two other schools that they were in noncompliance with a district-wide policy. The third point (and this was within the school and not stated unless I asked) was that not all of the teachers in the school were teaching the grammar or using the pre- and posttests. As the present chairman, who had inherited the system and the testing and scoring procedures, explained, "The kids come to me and say, 'Ms. so-and-so doesn't teach us the grammar' and I can go to that person and ask if she wants some help, but I could never go to the principal and report it." "Why not?" "Because she [the teacher] would find out."

This was the most extensive attempt I saw to revise and coordinate curriculum in either school. When I looked for issues to "follow through the organization," this was one of the first that was suggested. But what it illustrated was that a change in curriculum is initiated by an individual, in this case two individuals, and that the change goes only so far as those individuals' energy carries it. In the case of this change, both of the initiating teachers became administrators and the department chairperson left to have a baby, and at the time I was in the school the program was gradually drifting off. No one who did not have a personal interest in the development and continuation of the program did anything to change his behavior. The superintendent frankly did not believe in hiring supervisors. He was proud of the fact that of eighty-five school districts in the metropolitan area, his was eighty-third in terms of administrative costs. "We hire good people and leave them alone. Most teachers do a good job. It isn't worth the time and trouble to hire supervisors to watch the small number who aren't doing anything. The broad range in the middle, the sixty percent, they put out, they try hard, it isn't worth the effort to coordinate everyone to get at the few who fail." The director of secondary curriculum by his own admission had "spent the last twenty years hiring teachers and building buildings." He was at that time building a new junior high school, and he had neither "the time nor the staff to coordinate curriculum across four high schools." While one might blame him for not recognizing the efforts of the teachers or a few of the teachers, were he to do so he might have had to do something about those in other schools who were not following through. The principal, whom some blamed for his inattention to curriculum, followed the lead of the district in leaving teachers alone; besides, he and the assistants were busy with attendance, discipline, public relations, and personnel. The other teachers in the school, save for one typing and business practice teacher who complimented the English teachers because the students' skills had been increasing, paid no attention to the program. It was also interesting that while the suburban district maintained a very low administrator-teacher ratio and the urban district had a very large central staff and a much higher administrator/teacher ratio, the same kind of teacher autonomy and lack of coordination was exhibited there as was exhibited in the suburban school.

Other curriculum efforts followed a similar pattern. They went as far as one or more individuals' energy and enthusiasm could take them in schools where even those with ostensible authority over such matters were not allowed to intrude into what or how one teaches. With no institutionalized process for systematic implimentation or evaluation, then the individual(s) who wanted a change could create one and could even find some like-minded people to assist, but when her interest changed or enthusiasm faded or when the likemindedness no longer held, then the program ceased. And even on those occasions when the department did try to exert some influence, that influence stopped at the classroom door.

At an English Department meeting the staff gave further evidence of this unwillingness to let any collective effort affect their individual teaching. The main item on the agenda was "possible changes in the curriculum," but the discussion was desultory at best. Of the eight people present, one had herself paged out by the office, one was reading, two were working on their class papers but took a limited part, and the others entered and exited the discussion sporadically. Of grammar, one said they should stress it; another commented that without writing stressing grammar made no sense. Another commented on sentence structure, saying it was overstressed; another disagreed. No discussion followed any of these random comments. No conclusions were reached and the meeting drifted off. When they moved to choose the year's outstanding English student award, as soon as one student was suggested one would comment that the person had "taken the easy courses," or had "just chased grades" or had not been impressive in his or her class. No consensus could be reached about a student who was outstanding, so the decision was made not to give the award.

With a few exceptions, departmental decisions followed the individual. There was K.'s paper, G.'s yearbook, L.'s chairmanship, J.'s honors English, L.'s Shakespeare, M.'s debate. If two wanted to do the work associated with coordinating the basic skills testing, fine. If not, it just would not happen. An exception occurred when a teacher wanted an honors ninth-grade English, had it tentatively approved by the principal, but according to another; "She couldn't do that, it would foul up all our ninth-grade efforts, so we went to the principal and stopped it." I noted this event because I was trying to abstract out the principles of the structure, and I thought that one might say: "One could do what he or she wanted as long as it did not interfere with the efforts of others. If it did, there would be some action taken to stop it." But neither did that hold, as the following illustrates.

In Suburban High each of three young male teachers was involved in a number of activities. Each was popular with students and each created an advanced social studies elective, one in international affairs, one in anthropology, and one in psychology. They started these classes over the objections of the department chairman, whom they bypassed on the way to the principal, and over the objections of some more senior faculty members, one of whom simply lost his enrollment to those new classes, another of whom was left with five classes of ninth-grade civics. Each of these three young people rolled over the department, each created his own subspecialty and took it into the curriculum, each justified his efforts by asserting that the students "needed" his class.

I will return to that particular instance in order to discuss the relationship between the principal and the teachers, but the point is that there seems to be little in the way of restraint on the ability of individual teachers to create the curriculum the way they wish. A good portion of this can be explained in terms of supervision stopping at the classroom door. A social studies teacher in Factory High wanted to initiate an elective in geography and was refused, but he did not let it stop him. As he put it: "Now I get a map into every social studies class I have."

The fact is that department membership meant something only on occasions when one would find it convenient to use it to further his personal ends. When a teacher whom the advanced biology teacher personally did not like was assigned to teach elementary biology, the latter went to the principal and argued that the department did not want that person. But when in that same department the chairman wanted some cooperation for a departmental inservice, that same advanced biology teacher refused to cooperate, refused to attend the agreed-upon activity, and even took two other science teachers away with him for the day. When he wanted to use the department to protect his interests, he used it. When it was inconvenient, he ignored it with impunity. When the coaches at Suburban

High wanted increased supplies, they went to the department chairman and argued as a group; when there was an attempt to get them to participate in a departmental inservice designed to add some skills to their repertoire, they refused to attend the activities. The weakness of departments was indicative of the weakness of the chairman's position. The chairman of the science department said she would never again attempt to coordinate an inservice. The former chairman of the business department said she could not do anything about the behavior of some teachers. "I tried to get them to come to class on time and not drink coffee in class, but it didn't do any good." In fact, one auto mechanics teacher who had been a department chairman was removed by the principal from the position for "causing too much trouble. He'd go right into their classes and check their plans." Going beyond the classroom door was not something one did in the name of a department.

I described the efforts of the French teacher in the suburban school, but a German teacher in the same department did not recruit students, was not successful in subscribing her advanced or even intermediate German classes, did not take part in the ethnic dinners or trips, and, according to the French teacher, "doesn't do anything." The fact that she was in the same department in the same school receiving the same salary under the same contract was not the compelling element. She just did not give her job the same type of normative compliance. A Spanish teacher in the same department admitted that while he had been enthusiastically involved for some years, his interests were changing, his family was becoming more demanding, and he was no longer willing to expend the effort. Department affiliation, per se, was not sufficient to explain what went on in those schools. The important unit of analysis was the individual teacher.

There is an additional element here which can best be explained by referring back to the three young social studies teachers at Suburban High who bypassed their departmental structure and had their courses approved by the principal. It involves an explanation of the school's reward structure. As presented thus far, it appears that beyond the basic rewards laid out in the teacher's contract, that is, salary and benefits, the rewards of teaching emanate from being able to create the kind of curriculum and approach one wishes and to be able to build an affective relationship with some students. If one wishes to create something that requires extra resources, then she only had to enter the larger arena outside the classroom and politicize for the needed resources. But the principal controlled many of those, and it seemed that he was quicker to allocate them to some teachers than to others. As I saw it, he rewarded most frequently those teachers who assisted him in the task of presenting the school favorably to the central office and the public.

The three social studies teachers referred to before were quite active. They assisted with the sports, coached cheerleading, initiated the pom-

pom girls, ran the student variety show. One started the gifted program, another accepted the responsibilities for coordinating career education. They did not get paid for any of that, save their athletic duties; they did it because they "liked kids." "It helps when they see you in a different role. When you interact with them on a semisocial basis, then your classroom relations are a lot better." Agreed, of course, but in addition it helped the principal do what he had to do, which was present the school in a favorable light to the paying public. That was accomplished by highlighting just exactly what these men did. The activities were worth a lot in terms of public relations. The belief among the administrators was that the "paying public" was most pleased by having the students engaged in activites such as band, glee club, drama, sports, and so forth. Those activities brought the parents out. That could generate favorable publicity, and that was what the administrators bragged about when making public speeches. The principals (who could after all neither hire nor fire, pay more nor less than the agreed-upon contract, give neither more nor fewer classes to this or that unionized, contracted, and salaried teacher) rewarded those who helped them make the school look good to the public by giving them what had they to give: permission to teach their electives even over the objections of the department chairman and senior teachers.

One could hardly blame the principals in any of these schools. In the absence of any coherent philosophy, save that the schools "serve the needs of the kids," they had to make the school sound appealing. It was interesting to attend the parents' meetings of both schools and watch each principal explain his school in terms of the elements that I described as being idiosyncratic. The principal of Factory High, in his standard presentation, spoke glowingly of his schools' "advanced computer program," the "music as expression classes," and of having "one of the few schools that offer philosophy." In Suburban High the principal spoke of the gifted program, the career education program, an award-winning newspaper and yearbook, and a girls' sports program. Each was generated and sustained by the efforts of one teacher. The principals made it sound as if these events and activities were part of a "planned" curriculum, but that wasn't the case at all.

This issue of the importance given to activities by administrators was somewhat complicated. In Suburban High, where a great number of activities were maintained, a few teachers felt that the "activities mentality" was allowed to preempt more important elements and that an academic or more disciplined approach to teaching was actively disparaged. They had not forgotten that in the previous year, one of the more "academically" oriented teachers had been the target of an attempt by the principal to have her transferred out in favor of someone with less teaching experience who could coach cheerleading. As one long-time teacher who was particularly disturbed by the "activities mentality" explained, "It was a matter of popularizing the curriculum in order to sell the schools." By "popularizing" he meant giving academic credit for activities (e.g., yearbook, newspaper, student aide positions, cooperative education, and encouraging teachers to forgo academic classes in favor of running activities) or at least rewarding most those who were most active in that segment of the school.

This teacher talked about a time prior to 1965, when there had been a superintendent who valued academic achievement and encouraged the pursuit of academic accomplishment, but who had a limited view of schools and would close them at four o'clock, not letting anyone in the community use them without paying. This superintendent could not obtain an adequate level of funding from the community, was disliked and subsequently fired. "He was literally run out of town. They hated him because he was allied with the old power center, the Lutheran church and the farmers, and he had no feel for the changing structure, for the real estate and development interests who wanted to have some say in the schools." The next superintendent was "a man with a gray flannel head, didn't give a damn about academics but knew how to relate to people, made the schools the center of the community, popularized the curriculum, got everybody included and passed board issues. But in the process he downplayed the importance of academic achievement among teachers and students." As this teacher argued, one cannot popularize curriculum and maintain a strong academic program. This was a hard issue to follow, because he was the only teacher in that school who put it that way. When in my interviews with others I suggested it as a possible perspective, no other teacher responded affirmatively. No one was willing to either disparage the number or importance of activities or suggest that those teachers who engaged in them were more favored than were others.

It is certainly true that the administrators have their own reasons to value teachers who participated in activities because they "got along well with kids." They do not send kids to the office, do not cause scheduling problems because of their inability to get along or because students do not elect their classes. They support the activities, show up at graduation and the senior prom, take cafeteria duty when asked, and are flexible in their dealings with the students and the schedule. It is also true that teachers who held up a strong academic ideal, who demand homework, quiet, writing skills, who do not give good grades without effort are more likely to antagonize students and their taxpaying parents, have students avoiding their classes, and have conflicts which wind up in the office. This emphasis on activities seemed to explain a number of things, such as the somewhat casual hiring practices, the fact that some teachers, notably those more involved in activities, were more free to do what they wished than those who were not and seemed more likely to receive the principal's support. But it was a hard issue to follow, because one cannot dichotomize the staff of that or any other high school into "academically minded" and "activity minded" teachers. It was also true, particularly in Suburban High, that there was a high level of public support which was responsible for the high wages and excellent benefits enjoyed by the teachers. The teachers who enjoyed those wages and benefits would naturally be reluctant to express dismay at the popularized curriculum which helped obtain them. And too, most of the teachers in that school come from colleges of education where they had been taught that the expanded, open, and elective curriculum with a heavy emphasis on activities was just what was needed to serve the "needs" of the students. Few had ever considered another kind of secondary school.

In sum, in those schools people were allowed and encouraged to create their own curriculum and their own approach to students, independent of their colleagues or their departments. That system was given tacit recognition by administrators who selected out the individual programs that helped them portray their schools favorably, and to the extent that they could rewarded the teachers on that basis. One could always make his school sound exciting and dynamic if he talked only about particular programs, and that is what they did. No principal of those schools ever talked about the school philosophy or beliefs or adherence to some common goals; the schools were always presented as an aggregate of discrete and disparate activities and events.

The argument is that if one wants to understand curriculum, one has to examine hosts of things which tie back into the approach the teacher takes, an approach that is bound up not just with one's teaching but with one's life. Just as one was free to decide what to do in the classroom, one was free to decide how important teaching was in his or her life, and how he or she would integrate teaching with other important life-elements. From considering this, I began to look at the way people did other things, things that according to the argument could be said to affect the curriculum. For many, teaching was only one of a number of central roles. At Suburban High one teacher ran a driving school, one owned a bar, another a tax accounting business, another worked at a race track, one worked (full time) for the post office, another (full time) for the phone company, a few taught for the man who owned the driving school, a number taught night school, two repaired cars, one was a cabinet maker, another a welder, one raised dogs, another was a carpenter, one was a "folk" musician, another had a band, another was in politics, another built race cars, and two owned farms.

There are additional categories of jobs within the school. There were seven department chairmen, an activities director, and a union representative. Three business and industrial teachers also taught co-op education and were given some additional expense funds, an office, and a last period free to pursue their out-of-school contacts. Also, there were some professionally related out-of-school activities. Four teachers, one each from industrial arts, Spanish, business, and band, served as system-wide department chairmen, and four were pursuing Ph.D.s. Then there were the coaches, twelve in all, and three more who worked part time for the athletic department. Also, there were a number of female teachers who maintained the major responsibility for raising their children and caring for their homes.

At Suburban High, I itemized sixty-eight positions, including those within and without the school, sixty-eight jobs that this faculty of sixty-eight people carried on in addition to their teaching. But in many cases, one or more of these jobs was held by the same person. The athletic director ran the driving school and coached golf. The man who worked at the race track worked co-op. The newspaper and the yearbook sponsors each had growing families. The man who served as system-wide business department chairman was also in-school chairman and also worked co-op. The chairman of the industrial arts department worked as a cabinet maker. A man who worked for the athletic department also pursued a Ph.D. Another who pursued a Ph.D. also served as a system-wide department chairman. The one who raised dogs coached two sports. The head basketball coach worked full time for the post office. The activities director owned a bar, the tax accountant a farm. The woman who coordinated special education raised horses.

In trying to ascertain the genesis of curriculum and having come to the conclusion that curricular decisions emerge from teachers' individual lives, it seems worthwhile to note that while teaching was a serious endeavor, for many it was only one of two or three serious endeavors in their lives. For some I suspect, although I have no proof, it was not even the major endeavor. This matter of teachers having second jobs is not often mentioned in educational literature and perhaps should be left undiscussed here, save for the basic argument that what goes on in classrooms has to do with teacher's lives, that a large number of those teachers had second or even third jobs, and that the logistics of maintaining them impinged on their teaching. I am not saying that people were abusing their teaching positions, but even if they were I could not demonstrate it, there being no criterion from which to argue that any individual was more or less effective than anyone else. Those who had the most going on outside of school could and did justify their teaching efforts by pointing to the extra time they gave the school, the excellent personal relations they maintained with particular students, and the amount of their own time and money they gave to school events. Like everyone else, they argued even in the face of some criticism from other teachers that what they were doing was "good for kids." In fact, the man who had the most going on outside and against whom the most criticism was lodged, when one of his students became orphaned, had taken that student into his home until the student graduated from high school. One would hesitate to tell such a man that he was not dedicated to the welfare of his students. So I am not arguing that these people were doing more or less than others; but I am arguing that to understand the curriculum one has to understand the complexity of teachers' lives, and these second and even third jobs are a part of that complexity and hence capable of affecting the curriculum.

It was said that some central office administrators were upset about some of this and felt the individuals were neglecting their teaching responsibilities. However, when I asked, no one in the central office had anything to say about it, nor was any action ever taken to stop anyone. Teachers had their contract which allowed them to do what they wished after 2:30, and there was so little supervision that if a teacher worked on something other than his classes during his free periods, no one took any official note of it.

The people who were most heavily involved in outside jobs, knowing that they were susceptible to criticism, tended to be careful. That some teachers and administrators resented and suspected that the school was being cheated of effort and time that it paid for, did not suffice to bring the question out for open discussion. But that lack of open discussion was interesting to me because it reinforced my view that each teacher is free to decide what approach to take to instruction and free to decide what part the teacher role will play in his or her life. One might, like the French teacher and the newspaper advisor, make teaching the center of her life; or do as others, fulfill the contract and put available energy into nonschool endeavors. Just as the system as a whole had no way to make judgments about what went on in classrooms, so there was no way to differentiate the teachers who gave normative compliance from the teachers who gave less than normative compliance to their jobs.

There is a related consideration. While some might see the disparateness and the absence of normativeness that I have described as undesirable or even detrimental to the education of students, these teachers did not see it that way. They had entered these schools while they were young and finding the system open to any number of possible accommodations, used that latitude as each saw fit, even if it meant finding a second job to take up their excess energy or increase their earnings. Each had his or her life allocated, and while there was an occasional lament about the faculty lacking cohesion, as individuals they seemed quite content with their freedom. To change from such a system to one that might demand increased staff cooperation, or additional surveillance by administrators, or a higher level of normative compliance, might be very difficult. In fact it was difficult to get people to stay after the contractually agreed-upon leaving time or to get them to give additional time to school in the evenings. For the most part, they seemed quite content with the accommodations they had made.

There was an interesting side effect to this. To maintain two jobs was sufficiently trying so that those who did it, just as did those who needed outside resources for maintaining their particular curriculum, needed the support of the principal to help them. If one had an outside job and needed the last or the first period open, or freedom from hall or cafeteria duty, needed to leave early or come late, or needed an assignment that would enable her or him to come and go with more freedom than most teachers, that person, too, had to enter the larger social arena of the school and politicize for those elements. This was brought out one day at lunch when the assertion was made by a colleague that "the principal can screw you." "How can he screw you?" I asked. "You're tenured, contracted, on a uniform salary schedule, and you're all well regarded by the kids." But what I forgot was that they were enjoying lunch in a restaurant, which required having a double lunch period. The principal could have arranged the schedule so that didn't happen, but these gentlemen were among the most reliable in the school for helping out with extra activities. As the principal said: "I can always call on those guys; they always help me." And they did. So he rewarded them through his control of the schedule, the one means he had at his disposal. He let them have the double lunch, but he knew that he could call on them if he needed some assistance with an activity or event. However, he did have to fill a certain number of classes during fourth and fifth hour, so that meant some other people in those departments had to teach when they might have preferred to be eating. It was this that helped me understand the power of the principal. The coaches wanted the eighth period free to prepare for their after-school events, others would want to avoid cafeteria duty, others would want extra funds or an additional class, a department chairmanship, a free first hour, or a double lunch. The power of the principal stemmed from his control over the schedule and those other resources that individuals wanted in order to continue the life they had created or were in the process of creating in that school. To the degree that he could, he entered into a quid pro quo relationship with individuals, awarding one a department chairmanship, another some extra funds, or a free eighth hour, a co-op position, or a coaching job. What he wanted in return was the willing compliance and cooperation of those people for activities and events. He wanted teachers to enter into the spirit of the place, and what he had to encourage it was a positive response to those who behaved in a cooperative manner. He was accused of playing favorites, but he was dealing with a tenured, contracted, and mature faculty. He could neither hire nor fire, promote nor demote, pay less nor more, give fewer nor more than the contractually agreed number of classes. What he could do was support their private versions of the job. I could understand the criticism from those who said he "played favorites," but as he saw it he was using what little he had to create some cohesion and coherence from this highly diversified set of individuals and activities.

It was interesting to speculate that if one were willing to do just as the contract stated, and wanted no extra funds or the better classes or any favored schedule or free first or eighth hour, if one were content with fifth-period cafeteria duty and five classes of ninth-grade general math or civics, neither the principal nor anyone else could have any power over one. But if a teacher wanted more than that (and everyone whom I met did), then he or she had to enter into the general social arena of the school and cultivate the necessary relationships.

There is another issue being touched on here, one that is discussed little in educational literature but widely among teachers. When I examined a school and found a great many teachers taking time, energy, and enthusiasm and putting it into nonschool endeavors, it opened the question about the rewards of the profession. In all the schools I studied there was a high agreement among teachers that the motivated students, those who joined enthusiastically in learning what the teacher had to teach, were in the minority. In Factory High the estimate was that there were 200 to 300 among the 2,400 students who would take the harder courses. In Suburban High, for 1,600 students, the estimate was about the same, and those students were highly competed for. One was free to start his class and recruit his students, but many could recruit only those who cared about being recruited, for whom school was not simply a burden to be borne or a place to be with one's friends. The honors history course which one wanted to teach would be competing for the same students that others wanted for honors English, chemistry, band, physics, or calculus. This was true not only of academic classes. Teachers and counselors reported problems recruiting for the more demanding vocational classes. One may ask then whether it is realistic to expect teachers to engage normatively while students engaged only marginally. In Suburban High, the students were neither unfriendly nor difficult, but neither were many of them normatively engaged in pursuing academic interest, as evidenced by the fact that two-thirds of the seniors and half the juniors left as early as they could to go to their paying jobs.

"They're blue collar." "They're working class." "They don't care, look how few show up for parents' night." (It was true; both schools had one evening a term when parents could come in and talk about the children's performance, and while they were adequately promoted, few parents showed up, "and the ones that do show up are not the ones you want to talk to anyway." "They're the parents of kids that are doing fine.")"We can't keep them interested." "They have to have everything explained in terms of what good it will do them on the job." "Do they challenge you?" "Yeah, they challenge your right to teach them anything."

While it may be that the outside interests in many teachers' lives indicate something less than a normative commitment to teaching, so it was that the majority of students did not themselves give a normative commitment. "Why do we have to study geometry?" "Why do we have to read this?" "What good is foreign language or physics?" These were often expressed in class, and teachers responded in terms of utilitarian and monetary rewards somewhere in the future. But it is difficult to justify the pursuit of academic interests when one has only utilitarian rewards to promise. Few students saw the value of abstract positive knowledge. Their jobs, cars, dates, sports, and families were more important. While the rhetoric of teaching is often phrased in affective and normative terms, the fact is that for both teachers and students, life in secondary schools is much more mundane than that. It is small wonder that teachers as well as students seek activities and interests outside school.

TEACHERS AND TEACHERS

There is one more aspect of the teacher's side of the school which needs to be discussed: the interaction among faculty members and how that might have affected their individual endeavors. The faculty did not develop curriculum together, nor were they unified in any way. But there were attempts on the part of district administrators to have teachers work on some common issues. These occurred on inservice days, which were organized by central office people and had to do with topics of system importance, such as special education, career education, testing, or public relations. These meetings were designed to inform the teachers of the latest developments or sometimes elicit their support and cooperation. For those designed merely to inform, the teachers would listen politely, bored but at least moderately awake while being addressed by a central office person: "This information on career education is so new that even I haven't grasped it yet." But when the meetings were designed to elicit cooperation or change behavior, such as those on mainstreaming the special children into regular classrooms, or implementing the statewide testing program, the teachers exhibited open hostility. They were not at all reticent as they complained about the time lost by testing and the lack of validity of those tests. They were particularly resentful of the whole special education movement, which asked them to accept low-ability children into their regular classes and create individualized programs for them. When a school psychologist, himself not a teacher, came to Suburban High to tell them how to individualize their instruction so as to accommodate these students, he was openly ridiculed by the experienced teachers for his lack of understanding of the complexities of classrooms.

In Suburban High one group of teachers organized a betting pool. They sat in the back during these meetings and would pool and then pick numbers indicating times for how long the presentation would last. If one had a certain number that might be short, he would ask a question to stretch out the session to try to make the presentation's length approximate his number. That was a good indication of the interest in inservice days. In Factory High the inservice days were by contract apportioned out as teacher work days, and when on one of them the principal held a faculty meeting and then suggested department meetings, the issue was grieved because the teachers wanted and by contract deserved the time for their individual preparations. Given what has been described, this disdain on the teachers' part is not difficult to understand. The structure was such that they were left alone to figure out how to run their classes and how to get along with the students; they did it, and they resented elements which impinged on the way they did it. Not only were they resentful of special education, mainstreaming, and school psychologists who took students out of their classes, they did not like the endless time taken by the state testing programs and they did not like the assemblies which called students from class. They did not like being asked to think about career education, or tornado drills or public relations or any of the announcements that came from the principal's office. They did not like anything that interfered with what they did in their classrooms. From the teacher's point of view, the structure was bifurcated. Each had his world which he created, his student referents, his style and approach, all of which were neatly holistic. Everything outside his own classroom had its place as long as it did not interfere. When a novelty did interfere or when the attempt was made to make it do so, the intrusion was always greeted with at least suspicion, more often disdain, and if some pressure were applied, open hostility or insubordination.

There were also teacher unions, but at the time of these studies these had little to do with anything except salary and benefits, which in the suburban district were excellent, in the urban schools less so. There had been times when union activities were well attended but during our studies, all of that was in the past. At the end of one faculty meeting in Suburban High the current union representative was trying to hold an election for next year's representatives. He put forth a slate and before the vote could even be taken, half the teachers had walked out of the room and the rest were on their way.

There was also the matter of personal relations among the staff. When talking about teachers' interactions, I had to sift through innumerable instances and try to winnow out those that seem to have something to do with the school as an educational organization. I discarded the pleasantries, the tales, the gossip, the casual greetings and conversations and tried to observe and take note of those interactions that were stable and enduring, assuming that their stability and endurance was evidence that they served some purpose. There were two kinds of these interactions in Suburban High, where I watched them most closely. The first was the type mentioned previously, in which a teacher would purposely build a support system for his or her own personal classroom approach. The newspaper sponsor cultivated association with the principal, a vice principal, an activities director who could help with funding, a central office administrator who helped her acquire some machines, and the district curriculum director. The yearbook sponsor needed the principal, the activities director, the same vice principal, and some other teachers to help with various aspects of the project. For many teachers an important part of getting and keeping what one wanted to exercise one's approach to the job demanded that she or he cultivate certain associations outside the classroom.

The second type of interaction pattern was composed of long-standing personal friendships, of which there were many in all of the schools. In Suburban High there was a group of men who went to lunch together every day and had been doing so for years. The luncheon meetings, the camaraderie and friendship that went with them, were important to each man and were the reason that one of them stayed in that school. There was also a group of male teachers who met every day before school, each lunch hour, drank some beer with one another on Friday, fished and hunted together, helped one another pour cement or finish off an extra room. Daily meetings in the pit (a dingy office adjacent to the industrial arts area) were important to having a satisfactory life in that school. There were, of course, many other groups of this kind.

All these informal groups and associations were individually created for personal reasons. None was structurally maintained or structurally rewarded. Membership in any one was open and voluntary. One could as well join in the fourth- and fifth-hour euchre club in the lunchroom as he could the group in the pit, the teachers in the nonsmoking sixth-period lunch, the special ed teachers, or the group in the bar on Friday afternoon. One could, even if he was not a coach, make the coaches' locker room his hangout if he liked and wanted to talk sports. All of the associations were fluid and nonexclusive, open to anyone who availed himself and wanted to join and take part regularly. If one chose not to join this or that one, or none at all, there was no sanction, no gossip about him, nor was he regarded as an outcast. Nor could I ever determine that membership in one or another of these informal groups affected what any teacher did in his classroom. While these associations were an important part of one's school life, they were not allowed to intrude on his or her approach to curriculum and students. As Mr. T. said of his best friend in and out of school, Mr. L., "as close as we are, I've never been in any of his classes. I wish he would ask me sometime, but he never does." It is not that the teachers never discussed teaching or students. They did, but never in a way that suggested that they were either seeking advice or consensus on how to approach their classes. There was consensus of a sort, but it centered on the common agreement that what one did in class was her or his own business and others did not have the right to either publicly criticize or offer advice. The classroom approach that each used was his own creation. The informal associations were never allowed to intrude.

All these associations, the ones that were purposely directed to gain some support and resources and the ones that were designed to help one fill out one's life in that school, were personally and individually initiated and sustained. Some of these associations were stable and long-standing habits and old friendships, some were purely pragmatic, but both types shared a common genesis. Someone cared to put in the effort and engage in the activity. If he or they stopped, it stopped. And the groups did not cross over into one another in any predictable way. It was never the case that membership in one of these entities effected membership in another.

SUMMARY

Just as teachers developed their own individual style of "getting along with kids," so they developed their own individual style of instructing. They even developed their own content. What one did in the classroom did not emanate from some agreed-upon curriculum in the department, school, or district. There were all sorts of diverse and disparate activities going on all over those schools, all initiated by individual teachers, all coming out of some set of individual predilections. Each was free to justify whatever he initiated in terms of it being "good for kids." At the same time, there was a need for cooperative endeavors, particularly for those people whose approach demanded resources that could be gotten only outside the class. That gave rise to a considerable degree of entrepreneurial activity in the school. Some teachers, in order to sustain their class, manipulated certain elements in the structure that they needed to sustain their activities. Each had his personal "field" whence came his approach, for one a set of people outside the classroom whom he needed to sustain that approach; for another a set of students, past or present, real or sometimes hypothetical, that he needed to justify the approach. An additional element in this theme of individual field is the fact that the teachers whom I met had very complex lives, made complex by second or even third jobs as well as families. The latter is not surprising. But what interested me was the way the organizational structure allowed them to create their approach to education and the curriculum out of the complex web of their individual lives.

5

Conclusion and Discussion

INTRODUCTION

Some events and behaviors in three public secondary schools have been described with the intent of using those descriptions to abstract a model of their structure, defined as an interrelated set of events which turn upon themselves to complete and renew a cycle of activities. It includes the events and behaviors and also the logic that binds the events and behaviors into a coherent whole.

While different from one another in terms of time, place, and clientele, in many ways the three comprehensive schools were quite similar, not only to one another, but also to most secondary schools. They were all moderately large, comprehensive, had the usual organizational pattern in terms of staffing, curriculum, and instruction, and carried the standard obligation to take and instruct everyone who showed up. They also shared the same constraints in terms of funding, legal obligations, parental pressures, and public relations.

While this book began with the argument for a similar structure and the fundamental importance of the egalitarian ideal to that structure, the separate studies did not begin that way. Each was distinct from the other, each began with its own issues and questions. In the first study, we reasoned from the tenor of the times and from our own experience in urban schools that biracialism was not only an important element in itself but also was likely to affect other aspects of the school. Using biracialism as the central issue, our orienting questions were: What do black and white students do together in school and how do their interactions or lack thereof affect other elements in the schools? When pursuing those questions through the classes and corridors of that school, we began to see that issue, as difficult as it was, as only a part of the much larger and more pervasive issue of maintaining order and discipline. In fact, biracialism was too sensitive an issue to talk about rationally in either of our urban schools. One could not even publicly discuss its potentially good effects, such as increasing racial tolerance and mutual understanding. Its ill effects of increasing tension and occasions for violence were treated, but as part of the general problem of attendance and discipline. That general issue of discipline and attendance became the focus of the study.

The second study also proceeded from experience, in this case my own, and from some conflicting ideas about the rationality of educational organizations. Questions about rationality involve questions about the way important decisions are made and executed, so in that study the orienting question was, How does the curriculum get created and implemented in two secondary schools? I reasoned that since public secondary schools have few administrators and little supervisory assistance, the teachers would take the major role in planning and implementing the curriculum and that they would do this in cooperation with one another, formally or informally. Therefore, the genesis and execution of the curricula could be most clearly seen in staff interactions.

In both studies I used field methods of participant observation and interview. In the first, my primary associations were with students, and the study was carried out in the corridors, cafeteria, and classrooms or wherever the students were in the school. In the second, my primary associations were with teachers, and the study was conducted wherever they were, in and sometimes out of the schools.

The major purpose of field studies is not so much to resolve conceptual and theoretical issues as it is to sharpen them, and it frequently happens that an initial issue or set of orienting questions is changed after the researcher enters the site. Indeed, it is just the flexibility and the opportunity they provide for one to pursue different directions that give field studies their usefulness. In the first study, I began with the issue of biracialism, but over the months saw that for that school, the problem was not so much biracialism as it was maintaining order and discipline. In the second study my initial issue was teacher interactions and that did not change. However, the focus of the study did change because I found that the key to understanding the curriculum did not reside in staff interactions but rather with each individual staff member. The orientation then changed from studying the staff to studying how individual staff members, each by him or herself, generated, executed, and justified what each considered to be appropriate pieces of curriculum.

In following the issues through the separate schools, the common elements of structure began to emerge. The central concept around which that structure centered seemed to be the obligation of the schools to take, retain, and instruct all possible adolescents in the hope of teaching them whatever they needed to know to participate in the life of our society on a relatively equal basis. Just as it became clear that there was a common structure, so it seemed that the linchpin of the structure in all three schools was just that commitment to the egalitarian ideal. In other words, it is just because these public schools were obligated to attract, retain, instruct and "serve the educational needs" of everyone, regardless of inclinations, predilections, or abilites, that there emerged a structure which ultimately left each teacher alone to work out his or her own version of curriculum and each student alone to work out his or her own education.

SUMMARY OF THE ARGUMENT: THE MODEL

The argument is that the dominating element in the schools described here was their obligation to the egalitarian ideal. Each school was organized around an elective curriculum in which students were provided a wide range of courses and left quite free to select those they desired. The arrangement was such that not only were students given freedom to decide what they wanted to learn, teachers were given freedom to decide what they wanted to teach. There was an absence of consensus among staffs on how to teach, on what to teach, on how to personally relate to students, on how much of one's life and efforts should be devoted to the role of teacher, or on how to conduct oneself relative to one's colleagues. People not only behaved very differently, they explained their behavior differently. A staff member entered those schools and found himself assigned to a set of classes depending on his specialty, and perhaps also assigned to one or more other duties. But beyond that which was stipulated in the contract, one was left alone to work out his own way of dealing with students, select his material, work out his approach, and handle his classes. Between the diversity justified in the name of appealing to a large number of adolescents and the diversity brought in by individual teachers, the curricula were much broader, more varied, disparate, and fragmented than anyone realized or publicly admitted. There was some attempt to at least verbalize a coherence or rationale which joined the separate pieces of the curriculum, and if I had limited this study to discussions with the superintendents, curriculum directors, and principals concerning guidelines and board policy handbooks, I could have found some coherent explanation. But there are two problems with such an explanation. The first is the absence of supervision and the corresponding autonomy of teachers. Many elements of the curriculum simply go on with no official recognition. The teacher knows, the students may know, perhaps the guidance counselors who assist in assigning students to classes know what goes on, but it is not written anywhere. In fact, what is written may mislead one as to what actually happens in the classroom.

The second problem with the official rationale was that it was always added post hoc to whatever individual teachers contributed. First, a teacher created whatever she wanted as a piece of curriculum. If it were then necessary, in order to have it implemented in the classroom, she could carry on the political maneuvering to work it into the schedule, engaging the cooperation of others as needed. Whatever sense the innovation made came out of the teacher's opinions, background, or whatever. One could always add a reasonable-sounding rationale, post hoc, and that is what people did. But it was equally possible that the teacher could simply implement the innovation into her classes without notifying anyone. The official rationale, as misleading as it might have been, could accommodate only what was made public by the particular teacher. No one ever took any official notice of other matters which may have been equally numerous.

It was interesting to note that what I described as being the basis of curriculum was taking place during the time when the teachers in those three schools were receiving hours of instruction in setting goals, developing behavioral objectives, and outlining schemes for implementation. It was also interesting to watch the respective principals talk in public about their school's curriculum and boast of their outstanding programs, which, as I described, emerged from the personal predilections of one or another teacher who had decided to include that element in his definition of his school role. Locked in their roles as the schools' public apologists, the principals spoke so as to make things sound coherent, planned, and organized. They always talked as if the "needs" of the students were somehow identified and catalogued, and these programs and classes were being developed in response to those needs. But that is not the way the teachers or the schools operated.

When this pattern began to emerge and I developed the working hypotheses in that direction, I continued to watch carefully for occasions which would disprove it. I was particularly attentive to department meetings, school-wide faculty meetings, and union activities, all of which went on and all of which made some contributions. But it was consistent that none of these was allowed to intrude on what a teacher did or did not do in the classroom. Such a system allowed each teacher to take whatever steps he or she deemed fit to maximize personal utility. I never found anyone who was not actively engaged in trying to enhance his position according to his inclinations or to accommodate an outside interest. In effect, a teacher was free to use the available freedom to create a private version of the job. The schools' curricula were open to influence by any and all of those diverse elements, none of which were processed through faculty deliberations or added according to some larger scheme or set of educational ideals. The curriculum was the aggregate of the teachers' idiosyncratic approaches.

This great diversity and disparity is the first element in the model of the structure. The question is, How does that element interrelate with other important aspects of the organization? For an explanation, we have to go back to the first study and part of the second, wherein I described the extensive efforts that went into keeping schools peaceful, particularly the two urban schools, both of which had the potential for racial violence. Both served a number of students who were decidedly tough. In those schools, almost all of the administrative and supervisory moves were efforts directed toward maintaining order and attendance, and those efforts took precedence over other possible administrative activities. While both schools had a vice principal for curriculum, that person supervised the halls, classrooms, cafeteria, and activities, and when trouble occurred, was pressed into service just as was every other administrator. Whatever was going on was less important than "keeping the lid on," as they put it. I noted that the third school, which was not biracial and in which there were fewer serious incidents, also had fewer administrators, but there too, the chief job of those administrators was maintaining order. In other words, it is not so much that this problem occurred only in the "troubled schools." It was given comparable attention in the less troubled school also. Not only did the administrators spend their time on those matters, they also tended to evaluate other elements, such as the performance of teachers, according to their ability to maintain order. They tended to arrange other elements of the school according to how they contributed or failed to contribute to the maintenance of order. The outstanding example of that was the implementation in both urban schools of the five-by-five day, wherein the students were brought in early in the morning, given five periods of instruction with a few minutes in between and a fifteen-minute midmorning break, and released before one o'clock. There were no free periods, study halls, cafeteria sessions, or assemblies. No occasions were allowed in which violence could occur. The importance of maintaining order in those public secondary schools could not be underestimated.

There are very good reasons why a disorderly school is intolerable. First is the concern of parents for the safety of their children. It is no secret that many parents have removed their children and themselves from urban areas where they feel that the schools are unsafe. That certainly happened in Factory High. I had been involved in an earlier study tracing the flight of whites from another urban school district and found that white families who had taken their children and left the city for the suburbs were much less fearful for their children's safety than were the families who had stayed in the urban area and still had their children in those schools.[1] "People have to know that their children are safe here" was the way the principal of Urban High put it, and that was where he directed all of his efforts.

Almost as bad as disorder was a reputation for disorder, which could be gotten if a small incident were attended by the press and the TV cameras. This could lead to displays of public dissatisfaction with the school and the formation of citizens' groups to investigate the school. It could also lead to votes against school bond issues. Year after year, national surveys cite public concern over discipline in schools. The vulnerability of public school administrators to such public pressures has been well documented.[2]

Disorder was intolerable for other reasons, more internal to the organization. Schools are highly bureaucratic, with their specialized teachers, rules and regulations, policies and procedures, timed periods, requirements, and so forth. Such bureaucratic systems have little tolerance for disorder, yet they serve a clientele of adolescents among whom, particularly in the tougher neighborhoods, order is always problematic. The scales are weighted on the side of bureaucracy so the answer to disruption and potential disruption is to put extra organizational effort into maintaining order. Operationally, that means increasing the number of bureaucratic measures—rules, regulations, policies, procedures, and administrators—to an even greater degree. In the schools I studied, those bureaucratic efforts to control disorder were quite successful, and discipline, except in extreme cases, had been changed from a problem to a procedure.

But beyond the fact that people want their children safe and the fact that maintaining order among large groups of adolescents is always problematic and when unsuccessful can disrupt everything else in the school, is a more fundamental reason for maintaining order. Our system of free public education is legitimized by the assumption that acquiring positive abstract knowledge can be made interesting and appealing to everyone. Such knowledge not only gives each person a chance at social, economic, and political equality but further ensures the continuation of a democratic society where class and social lines are left open and fluid. Disorder among students not only disrupts bureaucratic processes and frightens the children of the voting citizenry, it may cause that voting citizenry to question the value of attempting to educate all future citizens or it may confirm the suspicion of some that the attempt to do so is futile. Disorder in schools can serve as proof to those people that such students, particularly if they are from the lower classes, do not deserve the chance that society is attempting to provide for them and therefore the egalitarian ideal should be discarded. But if it is discarded, the public schools as we know them have no place in our society.

Were the schools I studied to set some simple standards and throw out those who violated them, they would be discarding their version of the egalitarian ideal. It would be an institutional admission that for some people the ideal does not work. But it is a universal, not a particular ideal. If it can be admitted that it does not work for some, it can be admitted that it does not work at all. That admission would deny the basic premise upon which public schools are founded. It is that line of thinking that obligates the public schools to demonstrate every day that they can take all the adolescents that show up, even compelling those who do not wish to come to do so anyway, and maintain order, instruct them, and hence improve their chances for political, social, and economic equality.

The issue is complicated because it is not merely a matter of maintaining order, but also of maintaining order among many who would prefer not to come to school, or to come and receive no instruction. It was not that many were hostile or disorderly or provoked assaults; it was that many did not like being instructed in terms of positive abstract knowledge. That was not surprising to me, because in a number of schools in which I have worked, I have found a number of students with a zero gradepoint average. They are not particularly troublesome, but they do not attend class or they attend sporadically. They skip the tests, do not hand in the homework, and just do not care. School people are reluctant to admit this, because it makes them look bad and also because as hard as they try to correct it, the problem persists. But the teachers in these schools discussed it candidly, admitting they had many more listed on their class rosters than were there on any day. It is not just a matter of getting all students to come so they can then learn the material; it is a matter of teaching them to accept responsibility for being there. Mr. D. expressed what most school people believe when he said, "The important thing is to get them to come." That is why so much energy and attention is given to the matter of attendance. And, too, there are very basic legal and financial constraints requiring schools to improve their attendance. State monies are allocated on a per pupil basis. In Factory High, a loss of a student was a loss of $1700, and the loss of seven students was the equivalent of a beginning teacher's salary for one year.

In addition, there are the legal constraints written into every state's school laws requiring students between the ages of six and sixteen to attend school. Compulsory attendance is so deeply embedded in our consciousness that it is easy to forget its origin in the 1840s, when those trying to improve schools believed that if attendance were not made compulsory, then those who needed it the most would not attend. The Pennsylvania Board of State Charities reasoned that "it is precisely those children whose parents or guardians are unable or indisposed to provide them with an education . . . for whom the state is most interested to provide and secure it. It was the children . . . who preferred the pressures and license of vagabondage and truancy for whom education is most needed."[3] As Michael Katz further pointed out, compulsoriness was the other side of imposing taxes to support the schools. "Taxation represented a solemn compact between the citizen and the state"; the citizen contributed in order to protect his person and his property. The state compelling such contributions is under reciprocal obligation to compel attendance at school.[4] In the text of *Brown v. Board of Education*, it was stated as well as it could be:

> Today, education is perhaps the most important function of state and local governments. Compulsory school attendance laws and the great expenditures for education both demonstrate our recognition of the importance of education to our democratic society. It is required in the performance of our most basic public responsibilities, even service in the armed forces. It is the very foundation of good citizenship. Today it is a principal instrument in awakening the child to cultural values, in preparing him for later professional training, and in helping him to adjust normally to his environment. In these days, it is doubtful that any child may reasonably be expected to succeed in life if he is denied the opportunity of an education. Such an opportunity, where the state

has undertaken to provide it, is a right which must be made available to all on equal terms.[5]

The importance of maintaining order and attendance is not simply because state funds may be lost, the community dismayed, bond issues defeated in an election, or the bureaucratic processes upset. All of those are important, but beyond all of them, the very legitimacy of the school rests with its obligation to preserve the egalitarian ideal. That means getting all students to come, even those that don't want to, getting them to stay, and attend class regularly, even if they would rather be somewhere else, getting those that are repeatedly disorderly to try again to see if they can complete the required work. If they can stay in their seats, learn to hand in their work on time, take and pass the tests, put up with the deferred gratification, then they may through education make something of themselves and contribute to the larger society.

The first element in the developing model was the diversity and disparity of the curriculum, the second was the demonstrated importance of the preservation of order, the third and final element was the joining of the two. Simply stated, in the schools I studied, the diversity and disparity of the curriculum and the accompanying autonomy of teachers to create and implement their private versions of the curriculum can be viewed as a retreat by the school from taking any posture or stance which might have interfered with the taking, retaining, and instructing of everyone. Were the schools to assume a position requiring a uniformity of curriculum, standards of achievement, or consensus among the staff on how to conduct themselves and their classes, it is inevitable that they would have had to make judgments about and take actions against students which might have damaged those students' opportunity for equality. The school would not take the chance of damaging someone's opportunity, and would only with the greatest reluctance admit the possibility that one had already by his actions damaged his opportunities. The school people purposely discarded anything that could have put them or their institution in such a position.

The curriculum was opened to all the variations that the teachers added to justify a particular course or particular approach. One had only to argue plausibly that the students "needed" this or that material or approach. Supervision was cursory and limited mainly to those who were new or having some trouble, and the major criterion for adequate teaching was that one could demonstrate that she or he liked and got along with the kids. There were no moves by any of the schools and rarely were there any moves by departments to impose any uniform curriculum or approach or content in any of the classes. Teachers were allowed to exercise their prerogatives in their teaching, and some, however few, were allowed to do little or no teaching as long as they "got along with the kids." The district organizations, while they had people assigned to supervise or coordinate curriculum, did not allow such people to enter and take active roles in the supervision or planning of instruction. Their duties were limited to developing broad outlines, committee planning, public relations, and personnel issues. There was no consensus on the part of teachers, even in the same departments, as to how to conduct classes, nor was there any attempt at consensus or even any vehicle through which consensus could be gained.

One teacher might not like the fact that another refused to teach the departmentally agreed-upon grammer lessons, but there was nothing she could do about it. One teacher might not like the fact that another teacher was not doing much, was not even keeping her classes up, but there was nothing she could do about it. Rather, the important element was that there was evidence of instruction, some retention of students, and some degree of order, and that, rather than hinging on some agreed-upon educational perspective, rested on the teachers' liking and getting along with the students. Even those students who did not particularly like school and did not particularly want to be there, would remain and would remain in a state of order if they liked the teacher and felt that she or he liked them. The bottom line was keeping the students in school and in a state of order, and the way for teachers to do that was to get along with them on a personal basis and use that personal basis as the center of instruction. But that meant that the curriculum was always heavily laced with the teacher's opinions, approach, background, and predilections. As long as one "got along" with students, nothing was ever done to interfere with one's content or approach. It was only when there were disciplinary problems in the class (always phrased in terms of the teacher "not liking kids") that the institution, in the person of the administrators, took some action. That teachers could, and some did, abuse such a system by not teaching in the classes to which they were assigned or by putting most of their efforts into out-of-school endeavors was not sufficient to stimulate changes in the system, because any imposition of changes would have resulted in the beginning of norms and could have led to pejorative judgments about students, judgments which would open to question the egalitarian ideal.

In sum, I have attempted to abstract an explanation of the common structure of three schools. The conclusion drawn from the data was that the important elements in their structure were the diversity and disparity of their curriculum and the comparable autonomy of their teachers to create and implement that curriculum as they wished. Such behavior, while scattered and even appearing random, did have a common thread, a coherence which combined and interrelated that set of events. That coherence hinged on the obligation of the school to take, retain, and instruct as many adolescents as possible, even those who did not wish to be there and who gave repeated indications of it. The way to keep them and keep them in a state of moderate order was to maintain a system that allows and encourages teachers to do as they wish as long as they get along with students and as long as it can be plausibly argued—and it always can—that what they are doing is "good for kids."

QUESTIONS ABOUT THE MODEL

While the school's commitment to the egalitarian ideal is at the center of this book, my studies did not begin with that idea. I came upon it after a number of attempts to find a coherent way to explain the events I was observing. It was certainly not the only idea that was tried, and even while presenting and arguing for its validity, it must be admitted that there are some problems.

First the term egalitarianism was never used in my presence by any of the staff or students in the three schools. Staff members spoke of the needs of students, the importance of attendance and order, and the necessity of keeping students in school as long as possible. They avoided imposing any norms on one another, put a great deal of emphasis on getting along with and liking the students, and continually diversified the curriculum to find ways to interest students. But in speaking of their efforts, not one ever admitted to a commitment to the egalitarian ideal nor did anyone ever use a related term (progressive, liberal, democratic, etc.). Nor did they ever indicate that they were familiar with the historical debates about schools which centered around some of those concerns. There were comments from which one could infer the general character of their schools: "We have to take the kids they send us," or "We have to take everybody and keep them all happy," but there were never direct discussions of the school's role in society. The term "egalitarian" was implied but never directly stated.

It was not that the teachers lacked a larger sense of what they were doing. Many cared a great deal about their subject matter and genuinely wanted the students to share their interests in and curiosity about how things worked, in literature, in language, or social and biological forms of life. Coaches cared a great deal about having their teams win and equally about having students realize themselves through participation in sports. Business and vocational teachers cared about having students learn the skills they would need to perform future jobs.

This latter element, education's utility, was commonly verbalized by all teachers. They continually exhorted students to work hard at school because what they learned there would eventually lead to jobs, security, income, status, and material possessions. Literacy was necessary because without it one could not make application for jobs, read directions, or execute written orders. Promptness was important because it would be expected in the work place and one had better get in the habit. Mathematics was necessary because one might have a job that required it and one always needed it in his personal life to balance a checkbook, calculate interest and payments, prepare income taxes, and so on. Advanced courses were advised because they would help one go to college, which was necessary to build a professional career. Up and down the curriculum with few exceptions, teachers argued for the specialties from this vocational or utilitarian approach. In fact, one could develop a model explaining these schools around that concept. Not only would he have the teachers' words to support the case, but a number of other elements could be included. Within schools, it could explain the cooperative education programs, vocational centers, and the career planning that was done by counselors. It could explain the emphasis on minimal competencies and preparing students for work, the state emphasis on attaining "life competency" skills, and the general talk that central administrators used when explaining the schools to the public. If one listened to the latter group, he would conclude that the schools' main function was to turn children into producers and consumers.

But vocationalism, while the most acceptable form of discourse, was not sufficient to explain the breadth and diversity of curriculum nor the nonsurveillance of teachers by administrators and colleagues. It did not explain the reliance on and broad interpretation of the term "needs of kids." It did not explain the schools' obsession with order nor the weakness of the collective relative to the individual. It did not explain why students were allowed such freedom to pick their courses from among those available. In fact, when teachers spoke of education's utility, I was never sure that they, having sat through approximately ten years of inservice sessions on career education and the importance of "life competency skills," were not merely mouthing the most convenient and acceptable argument for education, instead of accurately describing their own perspective toward their efforts.

Beyond that, one has to take more than the current rhetoric into consideration when explaining the coherence of the structure. One could not sit through classes, talk to teachers, and witness events both in and about the school without coming to the question: Why do these teachers do such different things and then justify whatever they are doing in terms of it being "good for kids"? It did not matter what a teacher did or did not do as long as she could do that and get along with the students. The next question to ask concerned the basis of that getting along. Rarely was "getting along" a matter of teachers and students being commonly interested in the subject matter or in agreement about the end of the endeavor. Rather, it was based on good personal relations between the two parties. Since good personal relations emanated from the kind of person each teacher was, so the curriculum emanated from the kind of person each teacher was. Joining that idiosyncratically based diversity and disparity with the emphasis on order and discipline, I concluded that for the overall structure, the most important element was the hope of providing some sort of instruction for everyone, even those who repeatedly demonstrated that they were not interested in acquiring positive abstract knowledge. This hope, which I abstracted into the egalitarian ideal, as I saw it, legitimized the schools' role in society and solved both the internal and external constraints. While vocationalism was more commonly voiced as the schools' driving force, egalitarianism better explained the events and behaviors.

There is the further question of whether the staffs preferred the structure based on egalitarianism. Teachers spoke as if they would prefer a more meritocratic system in which the schools had agreed-upon norms and standards against which individual performance could be measured. The school could then become a repository of those standards, and people coming there would know they had to live up to those standards both in academic performance and behavior. Such a system would give the teachers a way to motivate students beyond appealing to their personal goals. It is hard to justify a demanding curriculum to a student who asks "why should I?" if both teacher and student understand that it is only his "I" that counts. But if the teacher has behind her some collective understanding that "this is the way we behave here," not only is the question less likely to be asked, but there is a better answer to it: "Because that is the way we do things." Such a system would make the school more a source of learning than a site for individual fulfillment. It would also give the teachers additional ways to control reluctant students. If there were some agreed-upon standards of performance, the onus would be less on the teachers to prove that they "like students" and more on the students to demonstrate that they can and are abiding by school codes.

A more meritocratic system might have to be accompanied by a more communal organization. "Meritocratic" accompanies community as "egalitarian" accompanies individualism. I think many teachers would have preferred that communalness as well. Some spoke almost wistfully of the absence of any common norms. Many privately disparaged the colleagues whom they regarded as doing little, and they wished there were some way to control quality in the institution. Or they wished aloud that there were more spirit, more contacts, more collegiality among them. In Factory High some spoke of the "old days in the old school where if the principal told us a teacher was having trouble, we would go right in and help the guy . . . we don't do anything like that anymore. I don't even see people who used to be my friends." The same sentiment was echoed in Suburban High. "We used to have these gatherings, husbands, wives, kids, and a former superintendent would sit there and tell me, 'we're a family here, that's what we are.'" Whether in former times there really was some collegiality in any of the schools, I cannot say. Perhaps it was just that in former times many of the teachers were younger and still setting up their social circles, or still single and therefore more open to social events. But it was certainly absent during the time the studies took place. There were friendships, to be sure, but while carried on in school, they were not school oriented. Overall there was a decided absence of common norms regarding job performance, academic standards, or common beliefs among the staff. And while it may have been age or marital status, it might be attributed to the fact that the schools as institutions had to continually retreat from anything like common norms and standards that might lead to making pejorative judgments about students.

The teachers well understood that the imposition of a communal and meritocratic system with norms, expectations, and possible pejorative judgments about nonachieving students would place many students outside the purview of the school and leave them only the streets, the unemployment lines, possibly welfare or even prison. They had seen enough real-life examples to bring that home, and they used that threat, as well as the appeal to vocationalism and their good personal relations, to control the more reluctant students. As an argument, the combination was reasonably effective, as evidenced by the fact that students accepted it and phrased their own efforts in those terms. The teachers accepted the social burden of "having to take everybody and keep them all happy," as one put it. Some might have preferred a different system but they accepted the one they had.

The other side of that was that not only did they accept the system; many had done very well within it. Most had established what they wanted in terms of classes and duties, had their in-school life coordinated with their out-of-school life, and were clearly benefiting from a system that left them alone to do as they wished. The union contract took care of many of the details. Were the schools to change to a more meritocratic and communal system, some of those who had the most going on outside might have had to restrict their activities. They might have had to stay for teachers' meetings, or become more involved in school life, restrict their outside employment or stay later rather than going right to work, or home, or to pick up their children. There were decided advantages to a system that narrowly defined the role and left them alone to work it out the way they wanted without interference from supervisors or colleagues.

While some might have preferred a system with a different sort of structure, most understood the necessities which bound their schools and in fact came to make the most of their situations. If "making the most of it" meant that there was little common definition of education, that was the price they seemed willing to pay. I never saw anyone actively try to change the structure.

A related question about the strength of the model has to do with the source of the major pressures that form and sustain it. Have the schools adopted the egalitarian ideal because people who run and work in them actively believe in its worth, or is it for them a passive value which has been adopted in response to various public pressures? The major pressure, of course, has been the increase in number of students. In 1954 there were 6,443,000 students in public high schools (grades 9–12) and in 1976 there were 14,323,000. At present and for the forseeable future, there are approximately 12,000,000.[6] The diversification of these institutions, as described, was an attempt to respond to these added students, many of whom were of a type that might not have attended high school twenty-five years earlier.

The diversification is supported by critics who view the schools as not adapting quickly enough in directions that are appropriate. Those who wish to have schools change more rapidly or who see them as deficient usually express their criticisms by accusing the schools of being highly inegalitarian. They see some schools as closed, narrow, rigid, overly protective of students, oppressive, middle-class oriented, imperialistic, and even racist. Variations of that theme have been expressed by radical critics, blue-ribbon panels of "experts," special interests, and always by school people themselves. The suggestions that accompany such criticisms are always phrased in ways that were discussed; that is, that the schools should be more open, inclusive, individualized, specialized, and diversified. And school people themselves have internalized those same criticisms and as much as possible tried to fit the school's structure to the suggestions.

Among critics have been special-interest groups desiring this or that particular element integrated into the schools and into the curriculum. In one state, the Parents of Mentally Retarded Children, a well-organized and well-financed group, had their educational program imposed on schools by the state legislature, which they pressured by threat of court action. Many professional school people were opposed to the provisions that the group advocated, particularly the requirements that they place "special" children in a "least restricted environment," which in many cases meant putting them into classes with more normal children. But having no legitimate or acceptable way of articulating their opposition, they were no match for the coherent advocacy group. As an influential state education department official told us:

> Matter of fact, there was a great deal of opposition to that from the school management, superintendents, and boards; but they found it difficult to speak out in opposition to it. You know, it's education and education is good. You can't question it, even though privately they were say, "Oh, this will be terrible, we'll lose our control," and it was parents and special ed directors who pushed that bill through.[7]

The school people could not portray themselves as opposed to giving education, which has been defined as a constitutional right, to handicapped children. So they simply diversified the curriculum to include special education, and provided teachers with inservice sessions to teach them to individualize their classrooms in order to attend to the diversity of students. In the process, the school people again affirmed their faith in the power of diversifying and individualizing in order to solve problems.

It does not seem to matter who the critics are or even what they want. The accusations always come out that schools are closed, rigid, oppressive, racist, bureaucratic, and so forth and the accompanying suggestions are that they be open, diversified, individualized, and specialized. The response of school people is always to retreat from anything that could be construed as normative standards. Blue-ribbon panels come up with the same kinds of suggestions as do special-interest groups. In 1979 the Carnegie Council on Policy Studies in Higher Education issued a report on the problems of the young and concluded, among other things, that part of these problems could be traced to the structure of secondary schools. To help combat high unemployment, boredom, apathy, ennui, or juvenile delinquency, they suggested secondary schools "break up the big monolithic high school and its deadly weekly routine" and "stop the tracking of all students"; "all programs should be individualized programs."[8] The report further suggested that schools release their hold on students and create educational programs which place the child closer to the workplace. It is hard to say just how much pressure is brought to bear on schools by such critics and criticisms, but the schools described here seem to have gone a long way toward doing just what was suggested. They had retreated from taking steps that could be perceived as imposing standards, or closing schools off from society, or tracking or being unsympathetic to the vocational minded. Operationally, that meant that they continually diversified and fragmented their structures as far as they could to accommodate particular groups and individuals.

To the list of critics one might add those who see the schools as an imperialistic tool of the dominant middle class out to ensure its own children the higher places in society and to relegate the lesser positions to the children of the lower classes and the children of minorities.

> The purpose (of schools) has been, basically, the inculcation of attitudes that reflect dominant social and industrial values; the structure has been bureaucracy. The result has been school systems that treat children as units to be processed into particular shapes and dropped into slots roughly congruent with the status of their parents.[9]

As Katz sees them, the schools do not care a whit for the needs of particular children, only for the retention and bolstering of an oppressive class system. He sees a structure that is not at all egalitarian; it is not even meritocratic; it is simply imperialistic. The same point was made by those who accused the schools of teaching black children to be second-class citizens.[10] It was the thinking behind those criticisms that led these schools to abandon tracking and further diversify their curriculum to find ways to appeal to low-achieving students. Along with that went the abandonment of any hope for district-wide or school-wide standards (beyond the minimum) because such standards could have been used to make pejorative judgments about poor students, black students, and particularly poor black students. What radical critics, special-interest groups, and blue-ribbon panels desire for schools was also suggested by many who advocated more progressive schools where the curriculum would be centered around the needs of the students, where education would be for life, where experiences would be diverse, teachers would be empathetic, and schedules would be flexible.

There is no denying that the major pressures in education for many years have been in the direction of increasing the size and the responsibility of the schools while weakening any coherent perspective they might have contained. The thrust has been to optimize the chances of the individual to make maximum use of the school to serve his own ends, or in the case of various pressure groups, their own ends. The schools described here were doing, or had done, just what the special interests and critics suggested. They had opened the curriculum to allow individual students to create their own version of an education out of the mix of opportunities. But the descriptions demonstrated a basic problem with the approach. It assumes that each student has either sufficient guidance or sufficient sophistication and motivation to take an active role in acquiring for himself some positive, abstract knowledge. There were many who did not and the school had no way to appeal to those students save with the teacher's cordiality. That teacher-student cordiality is a key element in my thesis.

The answer to the question whether the school people have actively espoused the egalitarian values or have been backed into them by various groups and pressures in order to argue for their legitimacy is probably unanswerable, because it too neatly dichotomizes school people from non-school people. Also, it presents the school people as too-passive recipients of outside pressures. Those in charge of schools and those who speak for them have always believed that it was the schools' duty to serve as many people and interest groups as possible, and they have used the outside pressures and the criticisms to support their efforts and to increase the size and the scope of their schools. Diversification and specialization has vastly increased the opportunities of school people for professional advancement, increased salaries, greater job opportunities, and in general, larger and larger institutions. Colleges of education have taken the same perspective. Each time another particular interest came to the fore (special education, bilingual education, gifted education, career and cooperative education), it was warmly greeted by colleges which were eager for the increased funds and the opportunities for growth and increased resources.

The same held true for educators at federal and state levels. Those areas have grown exponentially over the last twenty-five years because of federal policies which have regarded education as a means of neutralizing inherent or environmental disadvantages. No group of public educators at any level has ever seriously resisted the increased opportunities and resources that have come to schools and school people as a result. And no group has ever seriously resisted the accompanying fragmentation and diversification of the institutions that have accompanied those increased opportunities. While I believe that if left alone, teachers might develop a more meritocratic and communal structure, that has not been possible given the pressures. As it is, they are left with the conviction that what they are doing in those schools is indeed "good for kids," and too, they are avoiding the more serious charges of racism, imperialism, rigidity, sterility, and irrelevance. Even if, for some educators (teachers mainly), the egalitarian ideal is held as a matter of necessity rather than as a matter of belief, more useful for its ability to accommodate environmental constraints and pressures than embraced ideologically, that does not make it any the less real.

IMPLICATIONS OF THE MODEL

All that brings us to the question of the generalizability of the findings. There are certainly limits to analogical reasoning, but there is some justification for making the assumption that what went on in the three schools studied also goes on in other schools. That type of reasoning is stronger as the objects inferred from more closely resemble the objects referred to. Each of the three schools was, in its own way, somewhat special, but together they did share similarities among themselves and with other secondary schools. Two of the schools I studied were urban and biracial and all three were according to the teachers primarily made up of working- or lower-class students.

However, there are a great many secondary schools where the more difficult classes are easier to subscribe and where a higher percentage of students are motivated to take harder classes. One of the major features of the three schools was the limited number of students who would sign up for more difficult classes, even harder vocational classes. In the urban schools there were a great number of very poor readers, and in the suburban school, the number of juniors and seniors who left school as early as they could was an indication of their academic motivational level. There are certainly many secondary schools where the teachers may begin their instruction from a more congenial basis than in these three schools. The idiosyncratic approaches and diversifying of the curriculum may have been greater in the schools I studied just because of those particular students.

Not only does the class issue limit the analogy between these and other schools, but each of the three contained some unique features. The first study was done at a time when the black-white issue in that area was particularly troublesome, both in and out of school. At the time of the second study, Factory High's district was plagued by financial problems which helped to limit the schools' ability to sustain programs. The district wherein Suburban High was located had an excellent reputation for community support, but that support was gained by doing everything possible to please the parents. According to a few long-time teachers, that seriously damaged any efforts to present a more standardized and cohesive curriculum.

On the other hand, while each of these schools had its own unique features and while the three together contained some elements that could limit analogical reasoning, there is an argument that what went on in those three does indeed go on in other places. I reported diversity and disparity in the curriculum of three schools. So did Susan Abramowitz and her colleagues in their study of two thousand American secondary schools:

> Equally puzzling nonrelationships lead to the general conclusion that important aspects of the high school organization—administrative structure and rules and other mechanisms for coordination—are not connected to each other.
>
> And schools with more varied courses, credit options, and services also have a more complex and differentiated staff, which exercises broader participation in the school decisions. The coordination mechanisms we examined—the use of rules, evaluations, and meetings—have little to do with how complex the schools' instruction programs are. For instance, one might have reasonably expected that, in a school with numerous courses and nonclassroom arrangements, meetings and evaluations would occur more frequently in the interest of control. However, they do not.[11]

The schools I studied did resemble the broader description of Abramowitz and her colleagues.

There is a certain sameness about comprehensive secondary schools. They look alike. They all share the structure, the specialized teachers teaching their particular subjects to batches of adolescents for a number of time periods each day. They share the same administrative structure, the same accrediting agencies examine them for suitability, the same types of state regulations govern the teachers' certification and the students' graduation requirements, they are subject to the same type of public pressures, certainly the same types of legal, financial, and contractual constraints.

There are two questions: the first is whether the three schools I described are so sufficiently different as to discourage using the model abstracted from them to discuss other secondary schools. In my opinion, the answer is no, although the argument will be stronger the more those inferred to resemble these three. I certainly would not presume to suggest that what went on in Factory High, Urban High, and Suburban High goes on everywhere. On cannot do this limited type of field study and make such suggestions. That does not mean analogies cannot be drawn; it only means that they cannot be drawn by the same person who does the study and whose experience is limited to the sites described. A piece of research needs the active participation of both reader and writer. If one familiar with schools reads such an account and finds that what happened in those three approximates his or her own experience, the generalizability of the model is increased accordingly.

A second and more important issue is whether one may learn anything about schools by studying the descriptions and the model. If the events have been accurately described and integrated, and the model carefully drawn, one may use that model to ask a more general question about whether the picture that emerges is what we intended for those three or any secondary school. It is not necessary to make specific applications to other schools to engage in a discussion of whether this structure is acceptable, even for those three. While the data are site specific, they do reveal some of the unintended consequences of pursuing the egalitarian ideal through secondary schools, unintended consequences which must be considered when the total picture is drawn. One may discuss the implications of the descriptions and the model without generalizing the discussion to all or even most other secondary schools.

For instance, all one could conclude is that the sum of the system is such that the ideal of egalitarianism was actually perverted, and what emerges is a system that is not at all egalitarian. Those schools I described might have given up the right or the power to encourage their students to attain levels unattained by their parents, in effect doing nothing to give those from the lower classes the opportunity to move ahead.

Or one might conclude that the schools I described were just as "loosely coupled" as any number of secondary schools, and that loose coupling is quite functional, given the purposes and the environmental constraints on schools. Just as Weick, Meyer, and Rowan predicted, I found schools where there was a closely controlled superstructure and unexamined instructional system.[12] One could argue that the pursuit of the egalitarian ideal did not warrant the abandoning of the instructional process.[13] As I described these schools, despite brave talk about coordination and evaluation, the administrators leave the curriculum to the collective efforts of the teachers. However, the power that the teachers have is only as strong as that set of common assumptions that holds schools together as organizations. In schools, that set of assumptions centers on the differentiating, specializing, and fragmenting of the curriculum and the individualizing of instruction. Clearly, those assumptions favor the individual teacher over the teachers as a group. The reality is that these specialized teachers—equal in rank, pay, and union standing, isolated from colleagues, and unscrutinized by administrators—do not exert any collective control over the curriculum. Instead, they leave its creation, justification, implementation, and evaluation to individuals. Our argument leads us to conclude that despite all the talk about community and teacher/student participation, virtually no one or no group is in charge of those secondary schools.

Teachers, isolated as they are from both collegial and administrative influence, are left to their own devices as long as they "get along with kids," which, given the emphasis on order, is the primary task. They are in effect free to develop their own style of participation and compliance with the institution. Students faced with myriad electives in a largely unguided system are left to themselves to decide on the components of an education. Those with strong parental guidance and/or some sophistication probably make reasonable choices. But other students, particularly those from educationally disadvantaged families, may wind up with little or nothing. This kind of unevenness is a natural byproduct of our drive to make the schools "fit the needs of all the students," as the rhetoric goes. In such a system, both teachers and students approach the educational experience on their own; they are allowed to make of it what they will. Both the administrator's bureaucratic authority and the participants' collective moral authority have been permitted to dissipate. The institution, per se, has simply given up on any attempt to exert any moral authority relative to the student's education.

This surrender of authority raises some questions: Did we really intend, in the name of individual opportunity, to go that far in breaking up the schools; is it fair to confront a fourteen-year-old with important decisions about his education; in our haste to be responsive to individuals, have we ignored the very real educative power of a strong school organization?

Those questions were raised for me when at Factory High I found that of the entire staff, only one teacher sent his own child to the school in which he taught. The remainder of the staff had either moved out of the district, taking their children with them, or if they remained in the district, sent their children to private schools. It was true not only of whites but also blacks, teachers as well as administrators. In fact, while it was mandated that administrators live in the district, even the superintendent and deputy superintendent sent their own children to private schools.

Even more interesting was that being somewhat familiar with both systems, the private and the public, I considered the public to be considerably superior in terms of facilities, staff, supplies, and number of available programs. I frequently asked teachers why they did it, and the answers ranged from a few that were openly critical of the school ("I wouldn't sacrifice my children to a social experiment run by a pack of incompetents") to more general discussions of expectations, discipline, standards, and behavior. Those same people who talked about "fulfilling the needs of the kids," individualizing their offerings, and diversifying the curriculum were unwilling to subject their own children to the system. More than that, they were willing to spend money to send their children to schools that did not follow the system. The private schools in general were not nearly as well equipped, teachers were not nearly as well paid, and the options in the curriculum were much more limited. The teachers seemed quite willing to forgo those advantages in favor of having their children subject to some authority, standards, norms, and discipline which one can only conclude they found lacking in their own school. This was a hard issue to follow because it was a sore point with some teachers and many parents, and in general, the belief was that what one did outside school was his own business. But it does raise some questions about the worth of the structure presented.

It is interesting that many teachers chose private schools, where there is reputedly a somewhat different structure. Private schools have successfully presented themselves as learning communities wherein people have some common norms and standards and where it is expected that one will do more than simply care for himself; he will also take some responsibility for what goes on in the community. One is motivated, so it is believed, not only to work so that he can achieve relative to the collective norms, but one is also motivated to contribute to the well-being of that collective. Reutter et al. in *Fifteen Thousand Hours* studied some secondary schools in London and concluded that students performed better in those schools where the students resembled a group with common norms and expectations, and where teachers planned together, supported one another, and held mutual expectations for student behavior.

> Outcomes tended to be better when both the curriculum and approaches to discipline were agreed upon and supported by the staff acting together. Thus attendance was better and delinquency less frequent where courses were planned jointly . . . Much the same applied to standards of discipline. Exam success was more frequent and delinquency less common in schools where discipline was based on general expectations set by the school rather than left to individual teachers to work out for themselves.[14]

One might juxtapose Reutter's system and its normative elements cultivated and integrated into the system with the schools I described, where the suggestion of a normative element might be treated as if it were an oppressive and unnecessary intrusion into individual freedom. In effect, Reutter's school is closer to what Durkheim had in mind when he suggested that schools should emulate societies, because they are preparing students for society:

> Education is above all a social means to a social end—the means by which a society guarantees its own survival . . . that is the task and glory of education. It is not merely a matter of allowing an individual to develop in accordance with his own nature disclosing whatever hidden capacities lie there . . . education creates a new being.[15]

In Durkheim's model school the normative structure itself would serve as the important pedagogical entity teaching students the virtues of normative behavior, adherence to collective norms, and social responsibility. In contrast, the operating assumption that filtered out of these three schools was that the school was merely the sum of the students' and teachers' individual efforts. The major purpose of the overall system was not so much to facilitate individual achievement as not to hinder it from operating freely. One could see that in the rules and regulations. They were set up and enforced in order to iron out conflicts between one person and the institution or between two or more people who were having some problem, but they did not enable people to address school-wide questions. With problems always phrased in isolated terms, there was no avenue for an expression of collective approval or disapproval. In the instance of the student who assaulted the principal from behind, no teacher had a legitimate way to express the contempt that must have been felt. Nor did the

faculty as a whole have a way to regard it other than as a single and isolated incident, protected from moral outrage by procedure and legalisms.

One might defend the schools described by pointing out that
Durkheim is advocating something akin to Tönnies' *Gemeinshaft* type of
society, which operates best in a family or kinship group, where the idea
of an authority is the relation of the father to the child. But the prevailing
opinion is that the modern American secondary school has no place for
such paternalism. Schooling should be and is based on the rational exercise
of individual free will. Tönnies discussed those societies also, terming them
Gesellshaften.

> It [*Gesellshaft*-type authority] . . . can be derived only from the fact that the
> authority is based upon a free contract whether between individuals as a ser-
> vice contract or by agreement of many to recognize and place a master or head
> over them and to obey him conditionally or unconditionally.[16]

One could well understand why the schools would abandon the *Gemeinshaft* with its emphasis on paternalism, because there is always the danger
that paternalistic authority will be exercised whimsically or capriciously.
But that leaves only a rational type of authority wherein the participants
voluntarily submit to some kind of order for the purpose of achieving their
own ends. That type of authority can fail if the participants, or a sufficient
number of them, do not share the implied rational goals but are obligated
to be present for other reasons. That is what happened in those schools.
There was the rough assumption that if left alone to do as they wished,
the students would create a program which would give them maximum
educational return. But one would be hard pressed to demonstrate that
that was what was happening. In effect, the school could rely neither on
the paternalistic *Gemeinshaft* nor on the rational *Gesellshaft*, and was
forced back onto an increasing reliance on bureaucratic legalisms to define
the relationship between student and school, and a worn cliché, ("serving
the needs of each kid") to explain the relation between their processes and
their goals.

One could argue as well that these schools had also given up their
authority relative to teachers. Certainly the *Gemeinshaft* paternalistic type
of authority has no place in the relation between an administrator, who
may have been assigned the job primarily because of his ability to control
tougher students, and the specialized, contracted, tenured, and certified
teachers. One is again left with the *Gesellshaft* model based on the rough
assumption that if left alone and given the freedom their "professional
status" warrants, teachers will maximize the educational utility of their
role and take some active part in creating and legitimizing some authority,
an authority of the collective generated by their commonly agreeing to
unify, commingle, or coordinate their efforts, or at least agree to some
common norms. But that did not happen. Those teachers may have been
using that freedom to maximize their educational utility, but they might

just as well have been using it to maximize their personal utility. They were free to do as they wished. The rational model of authority does not seem sufficient to hold those school faculties together in any coherent way.

Other educators have supported the idea of building a more communal structure within schools. Erickson explained his findings about students in private schools doing better than students in public schools by suggesting the financial insecurity which plagued the private schools he studied generated a feeling of jeopardy, which motivates people to work closely together.[17] In fact, the sense of jeopardy generates the *Gemeinshaft*, which serves as the source of increased effort. Bidwell explained the superior results of private schools by suggesting that since students came voluntarily, they were more willing to attribute authority to the teachers, whereas in public schools one has to spend a considerable amount of time seeking to legitimize his authority prior to teaching.[18]

It is certainly true that for a number of reasons, including the findings of recent studies, the private schools with their proclaimed emphasis on a more communal organization do seem to enjoy advantages over public schools.[19] The question remains, however, whether their model is applicable to the public schools.

Following the study of Factory High and finding that the teachers and administrators were sending their own children to private, mostly parochial schools, I did a brief study of two such schools in the metropolitan area. Using field methods, I selected two small Catholic schools which in former times served a white ethnic population.[20] But the whites either left around 1972, when the push for school integration began, or if they stayed sent their children to the Catholic schools further out in the suburbs. At the time of the study, these schools were serving a 95 percent black, 60 percent non-Catholic student body. Briefly, I found many of the elements in those schools that I found in the public schools. There too, despite a lot of talk about community, there were teachers who gave varying degrees of time and effort to the schools. There too was a curriculum that reflected the individual predilections of the teachers, and there too were individualized and idiosyncratic ways of approaching students. There too was as diverse a curriculum as the constraints would allow, and there too teachers who wished students would read and write more clearly and join more normatively in pursuing their education. In other words, at the center of the organization those private schools were not all that different from public schools. I had no criticisms of those schools, but I was left with some questions of just what those school offered that enticed people to refuse the free public schools.

However, at the extremes of the organizations there were a few serious differences. One was exemplified when the principal expelled two boys whom the coach had seen take a football from the locker room and put it into their car. There was no hearing, no appeal process, no question about doubting the coach's word or his authority to walk out and take the football out of the car. "Brother can't stand a thief" was the simple explanation given by the assistant principal. Actions like that by principals of public schools I studied were simply unheard of. On another occasion, some football players left the school during the day and apparently went riding around drinking beer, and later returned to the school. The principal suspended them from the team and also suspended them from school for five days telling them, "You go home and sit by the phone and if I call and you're not there, then don't come back to school, and if I call I don't want any excuses about you being outside or in the bathroom." Simple, just like that. As he explained, "If I don't tell them that, it's just a vacation for them." Even more interesting was that during that same week, Brother admitted to the school a boy who had been expelled from the public school for carrying a loaded weapon and threatening another student with it. It was such direct actions, which those principals were free to take, that differentiated the public from the private schools. In that sense things were much simpler than they were in the public schools. It is not that people there did not have discipline problems. On one occasion a teacher was told "f— you" by a student and nothing happened to the student. After the principal-student conference, the teacher was told that "now he's calmed down." The teacher was just as irate over the student's action and the principal's inaction as any public school teacher would have been. What characterized their disciplinary procedures was the absence of universalistic criteria. Not only did those schools not have to take everyone, they were not obligated to treat those whom they did take in the same way.

The major standard was not so much an abstract set of expectations as it was a willingness to abide by the authority of the principal, which might be exercised one way at one time with one student and another way at another time with another student. Principal decisions were not wildly capricious, but they were sufficiently irregular as to make it difficult to pinpoint just what the rules were. The effect of such authority seemed to be that students were careful about what they did and said, more careful than were students in the public schools I studied.

The second interesting point about those two schools is that while there was talk about community among staff and students, it was difficult to discern just what that community was or what it did. Teachers did not agree on grading practices, teaching techniques, or discipline enforcements. In fact, they did not agree on the existence of God or the students' obligations to the Catholic church and the church hierarchy. There were interesting discussions around those points. One in particular occurred when a student asked if she, a Baptist, could receive communion. The pastor of the parish said no, the religion instructor said yes. The girl received communion. In other words, "community" was discussed but consensual norms were never pushed on anyone.

The private schools had some other problems. Their financial structure was precarious and, modest as the tuition was ($1,300 for an out-of-parish child, $1,100 for an in-parish child), many parents could barely afford it. Hence there were pressures on the staff to keep even the lower-achieving students in school, and they diversified the structure as much as they could to do that. Both schools had had a policy of admitting only those students who demonstrated they could read, write, add, subtract, multiply, and divide at a sixth-grade level, but during the study (1981), the pressures were on to lower the standards in order to keep the students. The schools were in a quandary because their reputations rested on the fact that their graduates went to good colleges, and they feared that letting in lower-ability students would cause their reputation to suffer. However, there was little doubt that they would stay open, because the second element that supported their survivial was their reputation for offering a "safe" atmosphere, which it was reported that the city schools were unable to do. As a parent related, "You don't understand; it's not a question of public or private, it's a question of which private. We won't go near the public schools."

Part of that safety might have been a function of the principal's power to intervene directly and personally anytime he wanted in any behavior problem. He explained it simply: "It's an authoritarian organization. That's the way we operate the church, that's the way we operate the school." Simple. And also simple was the fact that the parents who sent their children were quite willing to take the chance that authority could be exercised whimsically or capriciously. That did not bother them at all. In fact, when non-Catholic parents of Catholic school children were surveyed to determine why they sent their children to those schools, they reported great satisfaction with almost all the elements of the school, particularly the discipline and order.[21] Even more interesting was the fact that those parents did not see the limited finances of the private schools as a problem. Whereas the public schools have based their appeal on better facilities, increased teacher salaries, increased supplies, services, and options, parents who sent their children to schools with much less of all those things were not at all unhappy. We could only conclude that they did not see those elements as disadvantageous to what they considered an education.

But for all the talk about the private school model, there remains the question whether their structure is applicable to the public schools. The difference between the two structures is very simple. Theirs does not include the commitment to egalitarianism. They are not bound by the legal and financial constraints to take and provide some instruction for everyone, and they do not share the social obligation to take and instruct those who give repeated evidence they are not interested in the acquisition of positive knowledge. Their appeal is not difficult to understand. They were better able to demonstrate a coherence between their processes and their goals and could more clearly articulate a coherent educational perspective.

The private model is indeed appealing, and the presence of private schools along with some evidence that they are successful has helped foment a call for the imposition of some of their characteristics onto the public schools. A tightened curriculum, graduation standards beyond the minimum, a core curriculum, tracking, and tighter behavior standards are all being suggested as part of the new reform of secondary education. And indeed, all of that is fine, but a few points may be overlooked. The main one is that while the imposition of more concrete standards may be good for the structure and for the education of most students, such elements would demand that the schools make judgments about students, judgments of a type that the schools I described do not make. Many of those judgments would be pejorative, and many of those pejorative judgments would be lodged against poor students, black students, and particularly poor black students. It will be argued that such judgments are being made "for their own good," but it is unlikely that they will be seen that way. Rather, the schools will be opening themselves to the same charges that were leveled for so long—racism, class bias, imperialism, and so forth. There are some very good reasons why the schools I described were the way they were. Those reasons are still important. The other fault with the reform view is that people advocating it may not realize how deeply the structure I described is embedded in public schools. Teachers came from colleges where that structure was the ideal; indeed, the younger ones graduated from secondary schools where that structure was active, and now they work in and run their schools that way. Training in school administration has for years been centered around making the schools serve the community, appealing to "all" the students. Diversifying, specializing, and individualizing the curriculum have without question been regarded as "good" things to do. Those who oppose and speak of standards may be treated as opponents to progress or people who do not understand the role of the public schools in our society or even worse, who "may not like kids." There are some real problems with the schools I described, but there are some very good reasons why they are the way they are.

NOTES

1. P. Cusick, D. Gerbing, and E. Russell, "The Effects of School Desegregation and Other Factors on 'White Flight' from an Urban Area," *Educational Administration Quarterly*, 1979, *15*(2): 35–49.
2. G. Gallup, "Gallup Poll of the Public's Attitudes toward the Public School," *Phi Delta Kappan*, 1982, *64*(1): 37–50.
3. M. Katz, *Class Bureaucracy and Schools* (New York: Praeger, 1975), p. 47.
4. Ibid., pp. 45–46.
5. K. Alexander, *School Law* (St. Paul, Minn.: West, 1980), p. 465.
6. B. J. Chandler, ed., *Standard Education Almanac* (Marquis Academic Media, 14th Ed., 1981–82), pp. 96–97.

7. R. N. Nelson, "A Study of the Means by which the Michigan Department of Education Reduces Uncertainty in Its Environment," unpublished dissertation, Michigan State University, 1975.
8. Carnegie Council on Policy Studies in Higher Education, *Giving Youth a Better Chance* (San Francisco: Jossey-Bass, 1979), pp. 22–24.
9. Katz, *Class Bureaucracy*, p. xvi.
10. K. B. Clark, *Dark Ghetto* (New York: Harper and Row, 1965).
11. S. Abramowitz and E. Tenenbaum, with T. Deal and E. Stackhouse, *High School '77* (Washington, D.C.: National Institute of Education, 1977), p. 59.
12. K. Weick, "Educational Organizations as Loosely Coupled Systems," *Administrative Science Quarterly*, 1976, *21*(3): 1–19; J. Meyer and B. Rowan, "The Structure of Educational Organization," in M. Meyer and associates, eds., *Environments and Organization* (San Francisco: Jossey-Bass, 1978), pp. 78–109.
13. This argument first appeared in P. Cusick, "An Rx for Our High Schools," *Character*, 1981, *12*(7): 1–5.
14. M. Reutter, B. Maughn, P. Mortimore. J. Ouston, and A. Smith, *Fifteen Thousand Hours* (Cambridge, Mass.: Harvard University Press, 1979), p. 192.
15. E. Durkheim, *Moral Education* (New York: Free Press, 1961), pp. xi–xii.
16. F. Tönnies, *Fundamental Concepts of Sociology*, C. P. Loomis, ed. and trans., (New York: American Book Company, 1940; originally published 1890), p. 22.
17. D. Erickson, L. MacDonald, M. Manley–Casimir, and P. Busk, *Characteristics and Relationships in Public and Independent Schools* (San Francisco: Center for Research on Private Education, February 1979).
18. C. Bidwell, "Students and Schools: Some Observations on Client Trust in Client Serving Organizations," in W. Resengren and M. Lefton, eds., *Organizations and Clients* (Columbus, Ohio: Charles Merrill, 1970), p. 54.
19. J. Coleman, T. Hoffer, and S. Kilgore, "Public and Private Schools, A Report to the National Center for Education Statistics," annual conference of the American Educational Research Association, New York, March 1981.
20. P. Cusick, "A Study of Two Inner City Parochial Schools," annual conference of the American Educational Research Association, Montreal, 1983.
21. B. Gothard, "A Study to Explore the Difference in School-Related Values and Perceptions between Parents Who Send Their Children to Catholic Secondary Schools and Parents Who Send Their Children to Public Secondary Schools," unpublished dissertation, Michigan State University, 1982.

APPENDIX

Notes on Method

INTRODUCTION

The problem for the field researcher is to portray the reality of the unit under study, and in this Appendix I would like to discuss some of the issues associated with that task. In order to investigate the phenomena within those schools, I chose the methods of participant observation combined with interviewing. Field or ethnographic methods have been increasingly considered legitimate for use in educational research, and therefore I do not feel obligated to append more than a general explanation of them. However, I do wish to discuss some of the problems that I incurred, particularly in doing the latter study.

There are a number of methods useful for answering questions about human issues, and the job of the researcher is to select a method or combination of methods compatible with the logic of the question. This book was based on two studies, the first of interaction between black and white students in an urban high school, the second of teacher networks among the staffs of two high schools. The key assumption for both studies was that each school is in itself a social subsystem integrating key components. Following Parsons, the components of a social subsystem include roles by which one may differentiate members from nonmembers, values by which the members express an agreed-upon desirable state of affairs and norms which specify behaviors in particular types of situations.[1] These three components combine with a fourth, the idea of purposiveness or collectivity, to comprise a social subsystem.

Most commonly, it is just such a subsystem or some aspect of its components that serve as the unit of analysis investigated by ethnographic methods. In Urban High, we were asking about the norms governing the behavior of blacks and whites as they interacted or failed to interact with one another. We reasoned that those norms and the rewards and sanctions that surrounded them affected other elements in the school. Our conclusion is that they did, particularly the way teachers behaved in class, and administrators behaved toward teachers and toward other elements of the school. In the second study, I wanted to know about the roles staff members take regarding the creation and implementation of curriculum, and about the specific behaviors and the values regarding those tasks. Because of the similarities in the situations, in both studies we were examining behaviors in terms of norms, values, and roles in comprehensive secondary schools, and it was only natural that we should add to our considerations the element of collectivity and consider the total social system of those schools.

Participant observation is an appropriate way to undertake studies of social subsystems or their components because the subsystem is itself a participative venture created and sustained by the members as they pursue their endeavors. According to the logic of the method, the researcher must not only witness and describe the events under study, but by conducting himself properly come to participate in the creation and sustenance of those events. Ideally he will share the perspective of the participants, and come to understand the events just as they do. The result will be much more than a third-person account of the events; it will be a description and an interpretation of the events from the point of view of those who create and sustain them.

This reasoning follows the symbolic interactionist argument that since social reality is created, a true understanding of the reality can be had only if one will join in the creation.

> No one can catch the process merely by inferring its nature from the overt action which is its product. To catch the process, the student must take the role of the acting unit whose behavior he is studying. Since the interpretation is being made by the acting unit in terms of objects designated and appraised, meanings acquired, and decisions made, the process has to be seen from the standpoint of the acting unit.[2]

The researcher's success is contingent on his ability to access the events under study, take on the perspective of those creating the events, and describe those events from their perspective.

Critics of the method center their objections on the researcher's role. That is as it should be, because it is from that role that the description and the ensuing explanations emanate. Since the description comes from the researcher, who may develop an idiosyncratic role according to his own inclinations, then the description may be quite biased reflecting only the experience of that researcher. This is a reasonable objection and there is no way to answer it in the abstract. There are no specific rules of conduct by which one may assure the readers that the account he presents is valid beyond his own experience. A poorly done study will suffer bias and whimsy, but that is the fault of the researcher not the fault of the method. A well-done study will suffer from neither and will provide that accuracy of information and insight into situations that is desired. There is no theoretical way to assure the worth of any individual study. There are common-sense guidelines, but the worth of each result lies with the accuracy and plausibility of the description presented to critical readers who are free to reject accounts that seem laced with bias and whimsy. The obligation to present more than an idiosyncratic account lies with the researcher, but the test of whether he or she succeeded lies with the critical reader.

There are some general guidelines to be followed. One should attend the usual events as often as possible in order to familiarize oneself with the issues as well as to have one's presence taken for granted. One should do as much background work as possible about the history of particular events. One should develop working hypotheses and then pursue them systematically to see if and when they hold. In the beginning of the Urban High study, we frequently discussed among ourselves how little the blacks and whites had to do with each other, but when we followed that idea, we found that there were a number of occasions in which they were free to interact. In Ms. S.'s grammar class, on the few athletic teams that had both blacks and whites on them, and in certain activities, they did interact. What characterized those instances was the presence of a directing adult and a fairly demanding task. But when the task ended and the adult left, the taboos against integration were reinstated. Therefore, we modified the hypothesis. It also helps to test one's hypotheses by trying them out with certain people. Toward the end of the study in Factory High and Suburban High, I asked a number of teachers if it were true that they could do just about what they pleased in their classes. Invariably the answers were affirmative, and were followed by the reciting of additional instances which strengthened the hypotheses.

But gathering background information, following leads, and interviewing are only the supporting techniques. The central element in the method is the researcher's gradual taking on of the perspective of the participants, the sharing of their lives in those places to understand their world as they understand it, the adoption of the interpretations they use to make sense of events around them and construct their lives accordingly. To the degree one is successful in that, so he can describe the event and account for it just as would the participants were they to collectively explain their world. That is the goal of participant observation as a research method.

A second commonly voiced objection to the method is that the findings are ungeneralizable. Since such studies are always site specific, and since the sites are chosen more because they are accessible than because they are representative, then the findings may not be applied to other settings, even similar settings. There are a number of points to be raised regarding this issue. The first is whether an abstracted generalizability is a worthy goal of social research. According to Weber,

> general laws because they are most devoid of content are also the least valuable. The more comprehensive the validity or scope of a term, the more it leads us away from the richness of reality since in order to include the common elements of the largest possible number of phenomena, it must necessarily be as abstract as possible and hence devoid of content. In the cultural sciences, the knowledge of the universal or general is never valuable in itself.[3]

From Weber one could conclude that participant observation is among the most valuable types of social research just because it does include a great deal of site-specific information. That is its appeal. To suggest that research that does this is somehow inferior to that phrased in numerical terms may be to misunderstand the nature of social reality, as well as the nature of social research.

There is a generalizability to be had from these one-of-a-kind studies, but it rests not on the promise of proposition like laws, but on the general sociological assumption that since behavior is bound up with structure, then behavior that occurs in a particular setting may also occur in a similar setting. The schools I studied were each unique in some ways, but their basic organizational patterns were not unlike the general run of secondary schools throughout this country. It is not unreasonable to assume that the behaviors exhibited by teachers and students in other schools which are also comprehensive, large, organized the same way in terms of staffing and scheduling, and governed by the same general regulations would be quite similar to the behaviors described here. It is the obligation of the reader to determine if the descriptions presented in the account match his experience in similar places. If people familiar with comprehensive secondary schools agree that the descriptions are representative of their own schools or help them understand events in their own schools, then some level of generalizability has been reached, and as more agree, a greater level has been reached. It is not the duty of the researcher to argue for that abstracted generalizability, but to accurately portray the events in the selected site, adding a sufficient amount of information about the circumstances surrounding those events to make them intelligible to the readers.

There is a somewhat different view of the use of such studies. It can be legitimately argued that their chief use is not for generalizability, but for refining concepts that may be used for others in the future for more precise forms of research. That was somewhat true of our efforts. Although the selection of schools was in no sense random, that was not necessary given the purposes of the studies. We could argue that we were not trying to generalize the findings to a large set of similar schools, but to generate an explanation which would prove useful to others building more precise definitions of concepts to understand similar schools. The sampling then was not random, but theoretical:

> Theoretical sampling is done in order to discover categories and their properties and to suggest their interrelationships into a theory. Random sampling is not necessary for theoretical sampling . . . The researcher who generates theory need not combine random sampling when setting forth relationships among categories and properties. These relationships are suggested as hypotheses pertinent to direction of relationships, not tested as description of both direction and magnitude.[4]

With field methods, it is not necessary that random selection assure representativeness, it is only necessary that the phenomenon be present in the site. At the beginning of these studies, we had some orienting concept(s) and some plausible reasons for thinking that the events designated by the concept(s) were important to the participants and to the schools under study. In Urban High we had black-white interaction; in Factory and Suburban High we had teacher network. The studies were undertaken to see if those concepts were appropriate and if so to fill them out with descriptive material from which could be abstracted specific behavioral indicants and possible hypotheses. To some degree that is what a field study is, a lengthy effort to refine a conceptual scheme and to fill out concepts with behavioral indicants. The written report is an account of that effort. In that sense, it can support the work done by other researchers who may need more well-established concepts from which to formulate hypotheses.

However, field studies are not merely exploratory. The term "exploratory" is in fact misleading. It implies a cumulativeness or finality which simply does not apply to social reality or social research. There is no point at which everything of significance about some social situation will be known. Even a large number of such studies directed toward the same setting can never exhaust the possibilities of a piece of reality, "since a description of even the smallest slice of reality can never be exhaustive. The number and type of causes which have influenced any given event are always infinite and there is nothing in things themselves to set some of them apart as alone meriting attention."[5]

If one wishes to make the argument for field studies as exploratory, he may, but given the complexity of social reality and the fact that a given social situation can never be fully explored, by any or all methods, it is a weak argument.

It is better to defend field studies more simply. A field study, after all, is only an individual's attempt to unravel and explain a human event giving particular attention to the collective understandings of those who created the event. If the event is significant, and the account is intelligible and plausible, then the result can be of value to those interested and involved in similar events. While such a defense is alarmingly simple, to deny it is to deny that one may attempt to understand and account for the actions of others or that another may learn from a written account of that attempt.

ACCESS TO THE SCHOOLS

Our questions were about the exercise of norms, values, and roles within some secondary schools. The task demanded that Mr. Ayling and I in the first study and I alone in the second study have open access to all parts of the schools, familiarity with a large number of participants, and an acquaintance with important issues. As the methods are intensely personal, so is the means of access. In the study of biracial interaction, we selected a city which had a number of schools that fulfilled the criteria, and we then went to the research staff in that school district with the proposal. They said it was a good idea but expressed some skepticism about the implications and for a while it looked as though they would disapprove. Fortunately, it is not just a myth that administrators are ex-coaches, as is Mr. Ayling, and while I was trying to answer questions about independent variables (or the lack thereof) and tests of reliability (or their absence), Mr. Ayling was doing the important work. Passing by an office on the way to the researchers' area, he discovered an administrator with whom he had coached some years before. After talking awhile about some all but forgotten athletic event, they went upstairs to find more old coaches and continue that talk. In the course of all that, Mr. Ayling explained what we wanted and with the easy familiarity of old friends, they assured him that "it would be taken care of," the lack of independent variables notwithstanding.

The trust those gentlemen had in Mr. Ayling allayed the two major fears that insiders have of outsiders: that their presence will cause trouble, or that they will use their access to publicly criticize the organization. As the principal put it, "I can trust you guys, not like that bunch from the research institute [of another university]. They told me they were going to do a study to find out what 'was wrong with my school.'" That initial trust can assist one right through the study. Not only did the principal, another ex-coach, assist us by introducing us to some students who proved to be very helpful, but when one of us wanted some background information on some particular event, Mr. Ayling could return to his friends for the information.

In the second study I too called on some personal acquaintances, in this case two assistant principals whom I knew and who were highly regarded in their own schools. With the active cooperation of my friends, the necessary permissions from the superintendent, director of secondary education, principal, and teachers were quite easily obtained. Meetings were arranged, introductions made, informal discussions ensued, and the project was approved. Although one of those assistant principals had already been transferred to another school as principal by the time the study took place, their assistance was invaluable throughout. Not only was entrance facilitated, but throughout the study they assisted with introductions, helped with background information, and suggested further leads.

SOME PARTICULAR CONSIDERATIONS

The major consideration is what to do with one's own self. One has a physical presence. How will he fit it into the setting he wants to study? One has a way of interacting and some personality characteristics. With whom may he feel most comfortable? One has the problem of feeling somewhat useful, perhaps even needed. What shall he do with his energy and time in a place where everyone has some things to do while he has, ostensibly at least, nothing to do? If these considerations can be handled, one can get on with the business of listening, observing, and asking an occasional question. If those problems cannot be resolved, then a proposed study may never begin. For that reason, I would like to explain how some of those elements were handled in these studies.

In Urban High, the task was to affiliate with students while studying the element of biracialism. But the problem with associating with black students was that it made me suspect with whites, and the reverse was true if I associated with whites. My answer was to retreat from active participation and place a greater reliance on observation and interview. In the second study, the problem centered around the question of with whom should I associate. There were 68 teachers in Suburban, 101 in Factory, and among them were various cliques and groups and sets. One could find a group with whom to associate or one could just drift from associating with one group or individual to another. As I explained in Chapter 1, my preference is always to find a few people of like mind and manner, and make my primary associations with them and rely more on observation and interview for the larger group. Having a few people with whom one can talk and interact occasionally about the study but mostly about other matters, makes one more of a participant in the place, more of an insider. It can help make him more relaxed and less concerned with his own presence. It gives him a place to sit back, avoid calling attention to his status as an outsider, and watch and listen. After all, the study itself is seldom of that much interest to the actual participants in the situation. They are more concerned with getting on with the business that brings them there. While they will be polite and answer questions for a short time, the issues about which the questions are being asked are so familiar to them that such conversations are unlikely to hold their interest for long. And too, much of what the field researcher wants to know may be about things that seldom get verbalized, and by asking about them a researcher might antagonize people. If the norms of the place are such that certain things just do not get said, should a researcher say them, he would be violating those norms. By becoming very familiar with a few people, one may come to share their understandings of what does or does not get talked about. One can learn a great deal more that way than he can by asking questions all the time.

For that reason, one is wise when studying a fairly large social subsystem to find a few people with whom one can participate in the life of the place the same way they participate and keep the interviewing for those outside that circle. Such a move also helps establish one's identity. In any social subsystem of any size, such as the schools described here, there are cliques, groups, and subsets of all kinds. Everyone knows what they are and who is in most of them. If a new employee entered that setting, he or she would probably establish some friendships, and a researcher should do likewise. It gives him some added identification and further establishes him as one who within some limits can be trusted. So not only does finding some intimates solve the problem of what to do with one's presence, it serves the added function of establishing his identity within the setting.

There are problems, of course. Any subgroup or clique will have its own norms and expectations, which may be quite different from those held by the majority. In fact, inside small groups one will find a much more intense set of norms, expectations and values than one will find in the larger setting. If the larger setting is the unit of analysis, and not the small group, one can make the mistake of assuming that what binds the small group together is the same as what binds the larger social setting together. An awareness of the danger should help one guard against it.

The biggest advantage of finding some people with whom to associate regularly is that so many important events never become verbalized and never even come to the surface except in subtle ways. As one becomes an intimate he can become attuned to and understand those subtle ways. One of the more serious and subtly handled issues at Suburban High was the fact that many people had demanding outside interests, and it was suspected that these conflicted with their inside interests. Were one locked into survey or straight interview techniques (both of which depend on overt verbalization), one would not understand that because it was seldom talked about. But it was a serious matter. It was serious to the superintendent, who knew that teachers seen working outside could arouse community suspicion; to the principal, who was pressured by people who wanted some accommodation to the logistics of their lives; and to teachers, some of whom were making a lot of money outside, some of whom resented those who were doing so.

It was also important to my suggestion that teachers were generally free to create their own personalized versions of the teaching role. I reasoned that the genesis of the curriculum was the teachers' individual lives, and since these second jobs could be adding to the complexity of those lives, then I wanted to know something about them. But to ask one overtly would violate certain taboos. One does not simply ask another how much money he makes, or what he does with his spare time, or whether he is using the school's time to pursue private gain. It was a matter of serious concern and an issue worth pursuing, but one had to be careful how he pursued it. The best way to find out something about it was to keep quiet while it was being discussed and that required that one be sufficiently familiar with a few people.

It is not just a matter of finding out things that could be potentially embarrassing; it is a matter of verbalizing what people do, but which is so far embedded in the institution and in the minds of the participants that it never gets stated in intelligible terms to outsiders. In the case of finding out how people create curriculum, were an outsider to simply ask, he would be directed to the director of secondary education and given the standard curriculum guide, the one that teachers could or could not pay any attention to depending on their inclinations. It took some time and familiarizing before I came to the point of even knowing which questions to ask or of whom to ask them; only then could I begin to articulate the thesis that the curriculum followed the teachers' predilections. Those teachers knew it, but even they never said it, unless they were directly asked.

But one could not ask if he had not already established some insights into the workings of the school. Once those insights were obtained from the observing, the attending, the listening, then the question could be articulated. When I came to the point of putting it that way, the answer was always affirmative. When I came to share their understandings of the place, then I could phrase the correct question. That is the advantage of participant observation. Another advantage is that one may be permitted to attend to discussions where the workings of the structure are discussed by the participants. Such matters were being discussed at lunch one day. I interjected a simple question and my friend Pat replied, "It's like this, Phil, everybody subcontracts." That was the best statement I ever heard by any insider on how the school operated. An outsider can never arrive at such simple and direct expressions of what the participants share. But it is those kinds of expressions which not only give one the needed insights, they serve to confirm the insights one is already building.

A sensitive issue in Urban and Factory was the matter of race. People just did not talk about it. In the opinion of some quoted in Chapter 3, the subject could not be talked about without incurring the charge of racism or, as the principal believed, making the situation worse than it was. It was referred to but not directly and not often, and never in the company of people outside one's immediate group. If one were to learn anything about how this matter was handled, he had to be around long enough to be part of the informal interactions.

Lest the impression be left that the suggestions I just made are simple to carry out, I will explain how Mr. Ayling and I carried out the study in Urban High, and how I carried out the study in Factory and Suburban. At Urban High we wanted to know about black-white interaction, and wanted access to the places where it was carried out. It was simple enough to eat in the cafeteria, wander the halls, and sit in classes, all of which we did, but there were things that were not so simple. We wanted to attend the black literature and black awareness classes as well as the meetings of black students to discuss their possible joint actions. One would think, particularly at that time, that two over-thirty adults would have a hard time gaining admittance to places where black adolescents freely discussed being black in a white society. After all, no white teachers or white students were allowed in those settings. Some people in the USOE (which funded the study) were worried about this matter and probably thought it would be impossible.

I was not that worried about it. I had faced a similar question before when, as a thirty-one-year-old graduate student, I wanted to study high school students during the height of the rhetoric about those over and under thirty. Then, I found that the age barriers were easily overcome if I could simply learn to accept the behavior of the participants as reasonable and orderly.[6] I did not, after all, have to become a student. I had only to get my presence accepted so that I could observe them and interact with them on a limited basis while they were doing what they ordinarily do. It was no more difficult at Urban High, where the barrier was not so much age but race. The cafeteria conversation at the black tables did not change whether we came or left; when in the black studies class one of us was present, this did not prevent one or another student from saying that he hated and would like to kill whites. In fact, even those who said it did not look at us, or act hostile in any way; their hostility was directed at an abstracted whiteness, not at a particular white. I am not saying that they did not see our color, but I am saying that our color alone was not enough of a factor to change their behavior in any way. Nor did it cause them to exclude us from what we wanted to see. On a number of occasions one or the other of us was the only white in an otherwise all-black situation, that is, the cafeteria setting, the meetings to plan a black student union, the Harlem Renaissance and black studies classes, the Human Relations Day discussions. There was no evidence that our presence made a difference. We were not insensitive to the effects of our presence nor were our students reticent about saying what they felt. For instance, when I asked Mr. B. if I could sit in with the blacks who were trying to form a union, he said, "Well, you'll have to ask the kids . . . And they won't bite their tongues. If they don't want you, they'll tell you." And they would have—but they did not. But by the time I asked I had already gained some acceptance. Once previously, in black studies, the students were having a discussion and Herbie was angrily asking why blacks vote for white politicians. On the way out I told Herbie I thought he was making some good points. That afternoon the class resumed the discussion. (When these black discussions were going well, other black students from around the school would skip their regular classes and attend. These would frequently go on all day.) In his opening comments in the afternoon, Herbie made a big point of directing his attention to me, the sole white in the class, saying that "the man himself agrees with me." I did not wish to have any attention drawn to my presence, but I had to support Herbie and explain to the group just what I told him, about blacks being excluded from the political process. That took only a few seconds and I said nothing else. Later, when Herbie and I were talking about whites taking the black classes, he commented, "They can't do that; they're afraid they'd get killed. But they don't mind you. Remember that day you spoke up and supported us—what you said in class. Well, people knew you were straight and that you were supporting them right there. They don't mind you."

That they did "not mind" us meant that we could be present while they pursued the kinds of activities they were accustomed to pursuing. We were not trying to be personally close with them. We were not really interested in their personal lives, only their school behaviors, but they had to feel personally comfortable with our presence. If that is not obtained, then one can never put the people one is studying sufficiently at ease so that they feel free to act as they normally act when the observer is not around. To do that one has to be nonthreatening, nonjudgmental, present as much as possible, a good confidant and quiet.

In that school we rarely said anything, and when we did so, it was in a supportive manner. We did not ask personal questions except on rare occasions, we never bothered anyone, we only watched and listened. I have found that in doing this type of study, if one only listens and is interested, people will tell one most of what he wants to know. In some ways being white was an advantage. I would have liked to have included a black researcher in the study, but I do not think the absence of one made a difference. In fact, were one black he would have been dragged into the disputes that the blacks carried on among themselves, just as the black staff members were, concerning the way to accommodate the white institution. The students would not have allowed a black to stay neutral or mildly supportive. They would have forced him to choose his allies and make clear his position, and that would have been impossible for one trying to research a question.

As for those few extremely militant students, we consistently found that those who expressed the most hatred of whites, when asked for a few minutes to answer our questions, were extremely courteous and helpful. Frank, who was the most vocally militant student in the school, was quite helpful and frequently would ask me what I thought of one or another issue. He did not demand that I take his ideological stand. He knew that being white, I could not. Of course, the taking of a stand might have seriously impaired my effectiveness in other parts of the school. In fact, were I to become too strongly identified with one or another clique, and were some unpleasant event to occur involving that clique, I could have been asked to leave the school.

I am not denying there were sensitive and potentially embarrassing situations. I recounted how, after talking to a black girl one day in the hall, I was asked by a group of four black boys if I were "seeing that young lady." There was no mistaking the intimidating tone of the inquiry. I was in the stage of beginning to feel comfortable with some black students when, in the hall one day, I was talking to some white boys whom I knew had had trouble and been in fights with blacks. Passing by were four black boys, and as they passed, one said, "Are you black or white?" This was not a question. It was an accusation of disloyalty. I could not be open with both groups. On another occasion, I was going down the hall during passing time and almost bumped into a black boy coming toward me. He responded by grabbing my upper arms. I had seen this happen a number of times and the next move was a quick hit to the face so I grabbed him by the wrists. I could just see the study ending right there with me in a fight. We had a little face-down and he hooted and passed on. It did not end too soon; others were already coming over to watch. One incident like that and I would have had to leave the school.

The most sensitive issue was not black-white interaction, which was the focus of the study, but the question among the blacks on how to adapt to the white school. My access to this was through the discussions in the black studies classes, where they hashed this over and over. This was a whole new world for me, and I found their ongoing discussions to be very sensitive and intelligent. Accompanying those discussions was an open intimidation and ridicule of blacks who were considered too close to whites or too white themselves. There were many barriers to pursuing this; as one black girl told Mr. Ayling, "I have to be careful about talking to you, I need friends too." But we pursued it as far as we could within the confines of our whiteness and a study directed to other ends. As interesting as it was to a complete outsider, too much interest and involvement in it could have been harmful to the study. It could have involved me in some emotional issues or put me in the position of embarrassing some students in that school. It illustrated a problem with the method: When one does such a study, he wants to share the perspective of the insiders, but part of that perspective is their involvement in emotional issues. One wants to share the perspective, but he cannot afford to share the emotions because then he could lose his perspective toward his own study. With the many emotional issues floating through the school (e.g., white-black, black-black and class lines between groups), it did not do to get too close to any group or segment. There were too many barriers. The answer, as I explained briefly in Chapter 1, was to retreat from participant observation into a much more limited participation than I originally planned, with more reliance on observation and interviewing. It solved the problem of being too strongly identified with one or another group and being cut off from others, but it made the school a more lonely place and burdened me with thinking about what to do with myself when I was alone. However, for the sake of the study, it kept me out of emotional or potentially embarrassing matters. As the principal said one day, "You're not causing any trouble. If you were, I'd have a complaint or a grievance."

The study in Suburban and Factory was easier in some ways, harder in others. It was easier because the teachers about whom I wanted to know were about my own age, had similar professional experience. They understood it was a study of curriculum and structure and had little trouble talking about these topics. But it was harder in other ways. Teachers are busy between the time they come to school and the time they leave; they had something to do. I had little to do and I could not just go bothering busy people. My answer to that was to find some teachers who were like me; male, early forties, shared some similar interests; and see if I could share the regular things they did together. There were a number of groups. One

I happened on by accident went to lunch together every day, and I started doing that with them. In addition, I started hanging my coat in the social studies office, which was also peopled by teachers of my age and interests. Being around those groups regularly gave me an ease and familiarity with the setting, and from there I was free to see individuals, observe classes, interview, pursue issues in and out of the school, and attend meetings and social events. Gradually I was able to build a routine, which solved the problem of my physical presence and enabled me to pursue my study. But it was that familiarity with a few people that enabled me to do the other things. Not only did it give me some people to talk to, check matters with, and listen to about matters important to the study, but it gave others some way to "place" me within the school. That I was a friend of some gave me a certain identity with all. "Those guys you hang around with" was a phrase others used to me when discussing certain events. It happened that the people whom I knew reasonably well were quite respected by other teachers, and that may have helped.

Of primary importance was that I had some friends, some associations, some identity with a group, just as did almost every other teacher in the school. When I went to a faculty meeting or a social event or an athletic contest or anything else, I could go with one or more of them. When I missed something, I could find out what happened. When something was unclear, I could ask. And most important, I shared their informal associations, which served as my window to the way people behave normally in that school.

There was of course a problem, one that is too seldom discussed in the literature on field studies, the moral obligation one has to the institution and to the people whom he is studying. It is they whom he needs the most, they from whom he is likely to learn the most, and they to whom he has the most serious personal and ethical obligations. But it is questionable whether he can do them any good as individuals or whether he can do their institution any good. A field researcher is not a management consultant or a resource person for the institution. These positions would require that one maintain a limited scope of interest, confine his observations to formally designated objects, phrase his findings in acceptable language, and add a series of improving steps, also phrased in organizationally acceptable language. That is not the job of the field researcher. His study is not designed to make the particular site more efficient or effective but to unravel and explain the complexity of the events so that others who share similar circumstances may find ways to express and understand their world. At another level, the goal is to add some intelligent comment to the ongoing discussion of those particular types of institutions. My purpose in doing these studies and writing this book is not to "improve" the schools I studied. The purpose is to present a discussion of some American secondary schools' version of the egalitarian ideal. But when those people opened their institutions to me, there was an at-least implied assumption that the result would somehow do them "some good." Perhaps the findings could do some of the participants some "good," at least in the sense of adding to their own understanding of events, but I made no promise to return with an analysis and some suggested improvements.

For the institutional participant, the problematic element is the particular issue that needs resolution. For the researcher, the problematic element is the structure or the way that the participants create their lives in the institution. His problem is to articulate that accurately, not help to change it to suit one or another set of participants. His job is to unravel the relationships taking into account the full complexity and circularity and to make manifest unintended effects, not to serve as the spokesman for particular points of view or advocate the position of certain parties within the institution. To do so would be incompatible with one's task. Were one working for the institution he studied or for certain parties within the institution, he would be bound into articulating only what was convenient for that institution or those parties within the institution with whom he was allied. A researcher cannot afford to do that. He has to be free to present what Weber called "inconvenient facts—I mean facts that are inconvenient for . . . party opinions."[7] In the case of these studies, it might be inconvenient to have it pointed out that a school teacher may make a career of nonteaching if he can maintain some modest control of the students. For superintendents and boards of education, it might be inconvenient to have it suggested they have little actual control over what goes on in classrooms. It may be that one could mention such things in the institutions he studied, but if he did, he would be bound into making concrete suggestions how such elements might be purged or corrected. He would not be free to suggest (as I did) that such elements are an integral part of the overall school, not simply aberrations which might be corrected by more diligent supervision.

In Suburban High, some of the teachers reported that the principal played favorites among the faculty. A management consultant might try to help work on the principal's behavior or the teachers' perceptions to help solve that "problem." But my problem, taking both the teachers' perceptions and the principal's behavior as reasonable, was to describe and analyze the total event. I could understand the teachers' feelings, but I saw the principal as behaving quite reasonably given the limits of dealing with a mature, contracted, tenured, and certified staff. He had to use what little he had at his disposal, favors for people, to get the kind of cooperation he needed for extra activities and events. To explain it that way does not do an insider any "good" but it does what I want to do, analyze the event in terms of its complexity and its relation to the total structure.

A researcher's "problem" is to portray accurately what others see as a "problem," not "correct" it to one or another party's satisfaction. The conflict occurs when someone asks directly, "Now that you've studied the place, what do you think?" or "How can we improve?" To try to explain that is to take the chance of siding with one or the other party and "placing" oneself in a particular position relative to an issue. Not only would that make one a bad researcher, he probably would not be a very good management consultant, since that was not the original agreement under which he entered the institution. When such questions are asked of me, and they always are, I explain the findings and the analysis briefly and give the person who asked some attention while he or she responds. At the same time I avoid saying things that could be construed as critical.

At one time I did a study of high school students and reported among other things that they spent a great deal of school time associating with one another in their informal groups. My problem was not that they did it; that may have been a teacher's problem; my problem was to portray it accurately. I described it at length and suggested that it occurred because there was so little in the school that pulled the students out of those informal interactions. That explanation solved my problem, but it would not do to say that to a teacher or administrator seeking an immediate solution to that issue. That explanation based the students' behavior in the context of a great many other elements that could not be touched without upsetting the whole school, which no teacher or administrator was willing to do.

There does remain the sense of unfulfilled obligation to the institution or some of the participants. But I see no way to fulfill that obligation. One may discuss his findings with those in charge or those with whom he has some personal relations, and if they wish to pass it on or use it, then that is their business. If they do not, because they do not agree with the conclusions or because the analysis is "inconvenient" given their role, then that has to be respected. A field researcher begins his studies with the assumption that people are reasonable, that they do what they do for good reasons, and, were he in their position, he would behave in a similar manner. The participants in the institution have enough to do without being overly analytical about their roles or their world. A researcher has to respect that. His more important obligation is to the wider audience of people who are sufficiently removed from the particular site to be able to consider it in the abstract and then use the discussion for their own purposes. While this may fail to satisfy the sense of professional obligation the researcher feels toward those who opened their institution to him, it is probably the best he can do given the circumstances.

There is a second level of obligation. The first is the professional obligation of the researcher to the organization he is studying. The second, which in the case of participant observation is particularly troublesome, is the personal obligation one has to those inhabitants with whom one has come to share a sense of friendship. What kind of moral obligation does the researcher have to those people and is there any way other than by respecting the friendship that he can fulfill the obligation. Put another way, when undertaking such a study, one needs some friends within the institution, and the best way to find them is to join in with a small group. But that means respecting group norms, and a chief norm in any small group is that one will keep his mouth shut about confidences that are shared. It simply would not do to establish friendships with people, friendships in which genuine feelings are affected, and then violate the confidences that are shared within those friendships. Or perhaps it would do. Perhaps one could do it, but it is doubtful whether he could do it for long or do it with impunity. This is more of a personal problem than a professional obligation but unlike that latter, it has a solution. One may decide quite simply that while he needs the personal friendships to enable him to pursue the study, he does not need nor will he use the personal confidences shared in these friendships, even when they help substantiate the thesis. The result may be a weaker thesis, but that is the price one has to pay. In the case of this latter study, there were a number of conversations to which I had access and to which I contributed personal reflections, issues about money, about the rewards of the profession, about personal fulfillment in teaching. I did not seek out those issues and reflections as a researcher, but as a friend to that small number of people. Some of those conversations might have made interesting copy if I had kept notes on them. But I decided in the beginning that I would not do that and that I would not use private information, even to help substantiate the thesis. Not talking about those other matters, not even keeping notes on them, was my way to resolve what might be an ethical problem incurred by one who enters into friendships with people for the purpose of studying them. The unsettling element about the solution to both levels of the obligation is that while my solutions may not hurt anyone, there is the question of whether they help anyone. My answer is that the researcher's obligation to the insiders is to behave morally, in a manner that they would find ethically acceptable, and to take precautions to assure that neither his behavior nor any results coming from the study will harm any individual participant. On the more positive side, it may be hoped that his work will contribute to the general level of awareness about such institutions and that that will suffice for some "good" coming from the study. In this sense, the participants in the institution are also participants in the study who may also be said to be making some contribution to the professional field.

NOTES

1. T. Parsons, *Societies: Evolutionary and Comparative Perspectives* (Englewood Cliffs, N.J.: Prentice-Hall, 1963), pp. 9–11.
2. H. Blumer, "Society as Symbolic Interaction," in J. Manis and B. Meltzer, eds., *Symbolic Interaction, A Reader in Social Psychology* (Boston: Allyn and Bacon, 1978), p. 101.
3. M. Weber, *Methodology of the Social Sciences* (Glencoe, ILL.: Free Press, 1949), p. 80.

4. B. Glaser and A. L. Strauss, "Theoretical Sampling," in N. K. Densin, ed., *Sociological Methods* (Chicago: Aldine, 1970), p. 106.
5. Weber, *Methodology of the Social Sciences*, p. 78.
6. P. Cusick, *Inside High School* (New York: Holt, Rinehart and Winston, 1973).
7. M. Weber, "Science as a Vocation," in H. Gerth and C. W. Mills, eds. and trans., *From Max Weber: Essays in Sociology* (New York: Oxford University Press, 1946), p. 147.

Index

Abramowitz, S., on secondary schools, 121
Absenteeism rate, 27
Academic level of students, as problem, 64–66
Access, to schools, 135–136
Administrative structure, 24
Administrator(s)
  for attendance and discipline, 26–41
  and teachers, 31–34
Argument, summary of, model as, 106–120
Attendance, 25–41

Backgrounds, of teachers, 73–74
Biracialism, in schools, 13–25

Civil Rights Commission, state, suit filed by, 11–12
Classes
  cultural, social, and economic, range of, 22
  student, teachers and, 48–68
  subject matter of, 49–52
Classroom, as setting for student-teacher interaction, 49
Commitment, of students and teachers, 99–100
Common norms and expectations, Reutter on, 124
Comprehensive schools, definition of, 44
Conant, J., on comprehensiveness, 9
Confidence, public, 3
"Consensual basis," 22
Constraints, on teachers, 48–49
Contract, union, of teachers, 48–49
Cosar, L., on "non-realistic conflicts," 23
Creating curriculum, 73–100
Credits, definition of, 9–10
Cultural classes, range of, 22

Curriculum, 43–71, 72–103
  creating, 73–100
  and discipline, summary of, 111–112
  electiveness of, effects of, 75–76
  "established," 83–84
  of schools, 44–48
  "standard," 84

Departmental structure, 88–92
Desegregation plan, of city, U.S. Supreme Court and, 12
Discipline, 25–41
  and curriculum, summary of, 111–112
  problem of, summary of, 108–111
Diversity, as element in model of structure, 107
Dropout rate, 27
Due process, in expulsions, 35–36
Durkheim, E., on education as means to social end, 124–125

Economic classes, range of, 22
Education
  as means to social end, Durkheim on, 124–125
  utility of, 113–114
"Educational needs"
  definition of, 44
  and individual teacher, 80
Educational organizations, "rationalization" of, 2–3
Egalitarian ideal
  definition of, 1, 25
  at federal and state levels, 119
  obligation to, as dominating element, 106
  questions about, 113–120
Electiveness, of curriculum, effects of, 75–76
Entrepreneurial approach, 86–88
Erickson, D., and private schools, 126

149

"Established" curriculum, 83–84
Ethnographic methods, 131–132
Expectations, common, Reutter on, 124
Expulsions, 35–37

Federal level, egalitarian ideal at, 119
Finance, and expulsions, 37
Formal tracking, 46–48
Freedom, to individual teachers, 75

Gemeinshaft and *Gesellshaft*, Tönnies on, 125–126
"Good for kids," analysis of, 82–83

Human Relations Day, 18–19

Implications, of model, 120–129
Institution, obligation of researcher to, 143–145
Instructional system, Weick, Meyer, and Rowan and, 122
Interactions, "network" of, among teachers, 73
Interest
  of lower-achieving students, 65–66
  student, limits of, 68–70
Interview, as study method, 6–7

Katz, M., on purpose of schools, 118
Knowledge, positive, definition of, 5, 25

Limits, of student interest, 68–70
Lower-achieving students, interest of, 65–66

Martin Luther King Day, NAACP and, 17–19
Meritocratic system, 115–116
Methodology, for study of secondary schools, 6–7
  notes on, 131–146
Meyer, M., and superstructure and instructional system, 122
Model
  implications of, 120–129
  questions about, 113–120
  as summary of argument, 106–120
"Mutual cooperation," 22

NAACP
  and Martin Luther King Day, 17–19
  suit filed by, 12

"Needs," educational
  definition of, 44
  and individual teacher, 80
"Network" of interactions, among teachers, 73
"Non-realistic conflicts," Cosar on, 23
Normative structure, advantage of, 64
Norms, common, Reutter on, 124

Obligation, of researcher
  to institution, 143–145
  to persons, 145–146
Observation, participant, as study method, 6–7, 132–135
Order, *see* Attendance, Discipline

Parents, and teachers, 34–35
Parsons, T., and components of social subsystem, 131
Participant observation, as study method, 6–7, 132–135
Personal relations, among teachers, 101–102
  and students, 52–63
Persons, obligation of researcher to, 145–146
Politicizing, 98–99
Positive knowledge, definition of, 5, 25
Preparation period, of teachers, 49
Pressures, public, 117–120
Private schools, 123–124, 126–129
  Erickson and, 126
Public confidence, 3
Public pressures, 117–120
Public relations, and expulsions, 37
Purpose, of schools, Katz on, 118

Questions, about model, 113–120

Race, issue of, background of, 11
Racial animosity, "dealing" with, 17–19
Racism, 19–21
"Rationalization," of educational organization, 2–3
Researcher
  obligation of
    to institution, 143–145
    to persons, 145–146
  role of, 136–146
Reutter, M., on common norms and expectations, 124
Reward structure, 92–95

Rowan, B., and superstructure and instructional system, 122

Safety, 17, 108–109
School structure, 4–6, 104
Schools
  access to, 135–136
  biracialism in, 13–25
  comprehensive
    definition of, 44
    Conant on, 9
  curriculum of, 44–48
  private, 123–124, 126–129
    Erickson and, 126
  purpose of, Katz on, 118
  secondary, *see* Secondary schools
  structure of, definition of, 4–6, 104
Secondary schools
  Abramowitz on, 121
  studies of, 1–7
    methodology of, 6–7
  task of, 25
Social classes, range of, 22
Social end, education as means to, Durkheim on, 124–125
Social subsystem, components of, Parsons and, 131
Social ties, of teachers, 74
Special-interest groups, 117
"Standard" curriculum, 84
State level, egalitarian values at, 119
Structure
  administrative, 24
  departmental, 88–92
  normative, advantage of, 64
  reward, 92–95
  school, definition of, 4–6, 104
Student interest, limits of, 68–70
Students
  academic level of, as problem, 64–66
  commitment of, 99–100
  lower-achieving, interest of, 65–66
  and teachers, personal relations of, 52–63
Studies, of secondary schools, 1–7
  methodology of, 6–7
  notes on, 131–146
Subject matter, of classes, 49–52
Substitute teachers, 61–63

Subsystem, social, components of, Parsons and, 131
Summary, of argument, model as, 106–120
Superstructure, Weick, Meyer, and Rowan and, 122
Suspensions, 28

Task, of secondary schools, 25
Teacher(s)
  and administrators, 31–34
  backgrounds of, 73–74
  and classes, 48–68
  commitment of, 99–100
  constraints on, 48–49
  individual
    and "educational needs," 80
    freedom to, 75
  "network" of interactions among, 73
  and parents, 34–35
  preparation period of, 49
  social ties of, 74
  and students, personal relations of, 52–63
  substitute, 61–63
  and teachers, 100–103
    personal relations among, 101–102
  union contract of, 48–49
Teacher unions, 101
Teaching, in addition to other jobs, 95–98
Tönnies, F., on *Gemeinshaft* and *Gesellshaft*, 125–126
Tracking, formal, 46–48

Union contract, of teachers, 48–49
Unions, teacher, 101
U.S. Supreme Court, and city's desegregation plan, 12
Utility, of education, 113–114

Violence, 13–16, 37–38

Weber, M., on participant observation, 133–134
Weick, K., and superstructure and instructional system, 122